THE GOOD WINE

THE GOOD WINE

Spiritual Renewal in the Church of England

by

JOSEPHINE BAX

CHURCH HOUSE PUBLISHING
Church House, Great Smith Street, London SW1P 3NZ

ISBN 0 7151 5524 5

Published 1986 for the Board for Mission and Unity of the General Synod of the Church of England by Church House Publishing

Printed in Great Britain by
Burgess & Son (Abingdon) Ltd

CONTENTS

Cover photograph:
The wine is poured out by Pat Thomas.

The Alternative Service Book 1980

Collect for the Fourth Sunday after Epiphany

Almighty God,
in Christ you make all things new.
Transform the poverty of our nature
    by the riches of your grace,
and in the renewal of our lives
make known your heavenly glory;
through Jesus Christ our Lord.

FOREWORD

Renewal is a key idea in the Bible, part of God's design for created things. The nation and its worship, the individual, the Church, the whole of creation have an inbuilt principle of necessary renewal: *semper renovanda*. This theme of change and restoration underlies the great theological concepts of conversion, redemption and salvation.

But religion is also about what does not change and vary: God himself. The change and renewal in our created lives are designed to bring us to the unchanging, uncreated God. In a time of such rapid change as the present it is easy to grow shortsighted and become distracted by the change, either delighting in it or distrusting it for its own sake.

Josephine Bax aims to correct our vision. She has examined with care the way in which the Church of England is managing its changes at the local level and handling both the process and the idea of renewal. She shows why renewal is a practical necessity, and directs her readers towards its eternal significance. Her mass of detail reminds us that renewal means change 'from glory to glory', into the likeness of God.

RICHARD LEICESTER

INTRODUCTION

After the debates in General Synod on the Charismatic Movement in the Church of England, the Board for Mission and Unity was asked to keep under review the more general question of spiritual renewal in the Church. This the Board has attempted to do, and as a contribution to that process I was asked to do a year's research, and subsequently to write a book.

Spiritual renewal touches every aspect of Church life. Indeed, as Graham Chadwick said in an article entitled 'Imaginative Contemplation' in *Grassroots Magazine* (Jan/Feb 1986), 'Renewal in the spirit is something of the whole of life, because the Spirit of the Lord fills the whole world. It's to do with personal growth and renewal but it's to do also with relationships, with structures, with politics, with social issues and with everything that is in heaven and earth'. With the resources available to me, and in the time I was given, I can only begin to paint an impressionistic picture of spiritual renewal as I encountered it in the Church of England. One cannot measure what is happening inwardly to people in their personal relationship with God, but some of it can be seen reflected in attitudes, behaviour and relationships within the community. I therefore chose to focus my research on the 'coming to life' of lay people in renewal and their subsequent participation in the life, work and ministry of the Church, because this is such a significant aspect of today's renewal. But focusing on the laity also highlights the role of the clergy. I looked at present varieties of renewal and the nature of the spirituality that it evokes, in relation to God, the neighbour and society, with particular reference to the impact that it makes on the institutional Church; but the Church also reflects the state of our society.

I started by talking to a group of people who have either a national or a diocesan viewpoint. The vivid picture that emerged from them I checked by visiting parishes and communities, and by talking to individuals at the grass-roots.

In the time available I could only take a sample, but I tried to make that sample as representative as possible, spreading my net geographically and sociologically in order to look at different areas. I talked to people in communities that were experiencing renewal, and contrasted them with the experience of those who were not. I looked at the renewal movements, which are altering the Churches worldwide, so that although my specific field of study was the Church of England, I read ecumenically, and have quoted from writers all over the world where they seem to be addressing our own situation.

What became evident was a process that reminded me very much of my efforts, both disastrous and successful, at making home-made wine. If you have ever tried to make wine yourself, or have watched commercial wine-makers at work, you will have experienced the phases that the preparation goes through, and will know what care needs to be taken to produce a good result.

Having first assembled your ingredients, it is necessary to crush the grapes, or whatever fruit is being used, in order to extract the juice. This is strained, left to stand, and siphoned off. The juice is then mixed with yeast, and sometimes with sugar, in order to start the fermentation process. The yeast combines with the juice and the sugar to make alcohol, and gives off a gas while it is working. Care must be taken during this process not to let any impurities such as vinegar, bacteria, or mould spores get into the wine; if they do it turns sour or cloudy, which means you have to pour your would-be wine down the sink and try again. In order to prevent this happening, the vessels that are used must be sterilised, and the air kept out. Corking up the mixture too tightly, however, will lead to an explosion as the pressure from the gas given off by the fermentation builds up in the jar, and eventually bursts it open, leaving you with a sticky mess on the larder floor. The answer is to have fermentation locks, the home-made version of which is a cork with a tube containing a water seal, that lets the gas bubble out into the air but does not allow the air back into the jar. When your water seal is bubbling away, it shows that the fermentation process is at work. When the bubbling ceases it means that the process has stopped, and that your wine is ready to be drawn off into bottles. Most wine is better left to mature before it is drunk—and then, if you have managed the wine-making correctly, you will have the good wine that you can share with your friends.

   In the process that I saw at work in spiritual renewal, openness to renewal came as the result of personal or corporate crisis, which had the effect of opening up the situation and leading those involved to search for a way through their problems on a spiritual level. After a period of search, breakthrough was occurring as people came to realise the presence of God in the situation; there was an awakening to the spiritual dimension. But it is not a matter (as some in Charismatic Renewal have sometimes assumed) of just adding the Holy Spirit and stirring to achieve an instant solution. To start with, there can be no renewal without repentance, a *metanoia*, a change of mind, and the cleansing that follows repentance; otherwise what St Paul calls the 'yeast of sin' (1 Cor. 5. 7) will muddy the situation, or turn it sour. And the awakening is the beginning, not the end, of the process. It needs to be carefully handled by the leadership: those who have experienced the touch of God will need spiritual direction and the right employment and training, if the work of God is to bear fruit. Too over-directive a leadership can quench the Spirit and lead to a negative reaction. Sometimes clergy start the process of renewal in a parish, and then find the pressure that it generates too much for them and leave; like the too-tight cork in the bottle, they are blown off. A laissez-faire attitude on the other hand can lead to impurities getting in, and spoiling the fermentation. Bishop Richard Hare in the book *Bishop's Move* said that if the situation in renewal became bizarre he would look to the leadership for the reason. What is desirable is a strong leadership that can stand the pressure, harness the energy being gener-ated, and handle those who are literally bubbling with enthusiasm, giving them the right balance of training, support and direction so that the next stage of renewal is achieved, when the bubbling-over stops and the person is operating at a deeper level and beginning to be ready for ministry. Even at this stage there may be difficulty, because the Church all too often appears to be limiting lay ministry and not enabling it. There is also a need for the maturing process—which I saw very vividly in those offering themselves for full-time minis-try. Most of those I talked to who had had a 'landmark experience' of renewal and had been accepted for full-time ministry had waited for an average of five years before coming forward. Those who had come forward earlier than this were often turned down on the grounds of immaturity. Community renewal takes even longer, and requires sustained, steady oversight to produce good results. Two of the best examples of community renewal I visited had been involved in renewal *and* had had the same vicar for sixteen years. The mature person or community that had gone through the whole process without major mishap was the good wine that was being poured out in celebration and in mission.

This book follows the process through its various stages. The first chapter sets the scene and introduces us to the issues surrounding renewal. The second describes the challenge of crisis, the crushing of the grapes. The third chapter looks at the spiritual search that I observed. The fourth considers some typical examples of the awakening, and attempts some analysis of it. In the fifth chapter the impact of renewal on the Christian community is examined, particularly the role of the vicar, the 'cork in the bottle'. The sixth chapter looks at the different ways in which the Christian community is being rebuilt as the result of spiritual renewal, and is about the renewal of the Church for mission. The seventh chapter deals with liturgical renewal, and is about the way in which spiritual renewal is bringing worship to life. The eighth chapter consists of personal reflections and recommendations that have come to me as a result of this study. If I have passed too lightly over any one subject, please consider the size of my task and forgive me; any one of these chapters would easily expand into a book by itself. On the other hand, I shall feel that the book has failed if it does not stimulate the desire to go further and deeper into the subject than is possible in these pages.

This book, and the Spiritual Renewal Project that gave birth to it, would not have been possible without a great deal of help from many people who gave generously of their time and hospitality to me in my journeying. Unfortunately there are so many that I cannot mention them by name, but I should nevertheless like to thank them, particularly General Synod staff in Church House, Westminster, and the Diocesan Missioners for their contribution, and bishops, clergy, religious, and lay people from all over the country who shared their experiences with me. I should also like to thank the Central Church Fund, the Jerusalem Trust, the Sarum St Michael Educational Foundation, the Board for Mission and Unity and the Society of St John the Evangelist for their financial support. It has been an immensely enriching experience to undertake this Project, and I hope that this book may begin to give back to the Church some of the richness that I have received. I am aware that it is impossible to do justice to the subject in one short book, but can only offer the inadequate water of my efforts, and pray to the Lord to change it into the good wine, which will encourage, refresh and challenge the Church by its account of his work among us.

Josephine Bax

Chapter One

SETTING THE SCENE

What is renewal? What criteria do we use in saying whether or not a church congregation, a cell group, or a person is renewed? During my research I have heard comments such as 'The parishes that *think* they are renewed', 'Such and such a group talks of renewal but . . .'

Charismatics use the word 'Renewal' to mean 'Charismatic Renewal'; others who are broadly sympathetic with the Charismatic Movement but who wish to distance themselves from some of its extreme characteristics, use the word 'Renewal' instead of 'Charismatic Renewal'.

Both the Charismatic Movement and the Cursillo Movement have come to us from the United States, and have a considerable American input. Cursillo is Spanish for a 'short course'; the movement is based on an intensive short course lasting three days, which aims to give lay people an experience of spiritual renewal, and trains them for mission.

'Renewal' is used by some Anglo-Catholics and Evangelicals to mean 'a return to fundamentals', that is to say renewal by a return to the Oxford Movement or by re-establishing the fundamental authority of the Scriptures. Renewal is seen by others to be the result of

1

ecumenism. Involvement with Christians of other traditions produces a better appreciation of one's own position, as well as a vision of the Church wider than one's own denomination. Radicals believe that renewal comes through involvement in the main issues that face society—racial disharmony, poverty, unemployment, and so on. By facing these issues and identifying their theological implications the relevance of the Gospel is recognised and comes to life, bringing renewal with it. ('Radical renewal' in the context of this book is taken to mean the coming together of spirituality and social action which is happening today.) Liturgical renewal is helping to bring new life to our worship. The publication of *The Alternative Service Book* was a major piece of work intended to bring worship into line not only with modern language but also with new theological understandings. A curate, commenting on renewal and the healing ministry, defined renewal thus: 'It seems to me that a lot of the renewal has actually been about believing again that God really does do things, and that we don't just go through the motions and then carry on as if nothing has happened, nothing has changed; and healing seems to be one aspect of that, that God really wants to heal people, and really does heal them. We have got past the point of just giving the nod, and have started to explore it properly again.' The Meditation Movement is an emergence into the mainstream of Church life of contemplative spirituality which was once the preserve of the monastic. It has not yet been sufficiently recognised by the Church, but has a quiet yet important influence on contemporary spirituality and renewal.

For the purpose of this study the principal term that has been used is *Spiritual Renewal*, and the criterion that has been used is *relationship*. One cannot measure what is happening inwardly to a person or a group, or take their spiritual temperature; but one can see the shifts in attitudes and relationships that take place as a result of renewal. God, the neighbour, and society are the three points of reality through which we turn. Renewal in relationship to God is a key that turns the lock in the door and progressively opens us up to renewal in our relationship to our neighbour and to society.

If we look at some biblical material, we can see from Psalm 51 (which is a prayer for renewal) that renewal is a movement in penitence and faith from sin to holiness, from disobedience to surrender, from brokenness to joy and praise in the presence of God and in possession of his Holy Spirit; then, from the restoration of an individual's relationship with God, the Psalm moves to the building up of a community which gives acceptable sacrifices to God. In the New Testament, the word *renew* or *renewal* occurs four times. In Rom. 12. 2 renewal is a *metanoia*, a change of mind, from the acceptance of wordly standards to knowing the will of God. This is in the context of a life consecrated to God and to his service, from which flows a mutuality in relationships within the body of Christ. In 2 Cor. 4. 16 renewal is something constant and ongoing. Our physical body is dying, but our spiritual body is being renewed and will bring us to a new life in heaven. Eph. 4. 23 speaks of the new mind, heart and self that are created in the likeness of God, and which show in holiness of life. The death of the old self must be followed by the putting on of the new self, and this shows in the reformation of our behaviour to our neighbour. In Col. 3. 10 the new being is constantly being renewed by God so that we can know him. The old self has been put off and the new self, which is in the image of God, has been put on. As a result the barriers that divide us in society have been broken down.

In these passages renewal is a submission to God in

penitence, and a surrender to his will, so that heart, mind and spirit can be constantly renewed in his likeness in order to know and worship him. It is clear from the context of the biblical material that the reference is to a new walk with God, to a changed relationship with him, which in turn affects behaviour towards the neighbour and in society.

But we are renewed not primarily as we turn to God, but as God the Holy Trinity turns to us. 'Turn the light of thy countenance upon us, and we shall be whole' (Psalm 80). The initiative is God's, and the work of renewal is the work of the Trinity. As God the Holy Trinity renews the covenant relationship made with the people of God, our relationships take on, even though as in a distorting mirror, something of the nature of the Trinity. As the persons of the Trinity turn each to the others in mutual joy, self-giving, and love, so one may expect to see in a renewed person, group, or church, a greater mutuality and understanding of the giftedness of each other, a complementary ministry to one another and to the world outside the group, a greater love and joy, and new patterns of relatedness and work which not only revitalise but also alter the basic Church structure. While God was seen as a seventeenth-century monarch with his court, it was hardly surprising that the Church's structure should follow this model. But today's renewed structures flow from a very different understanding and experience of the Trinity. The Rev. Robin Green, Vicar of St Mary the Boltons, London diocese, says: 'Today people are searching for a new vocabulary of belonging. We are afraid on the one hand of loneliness, and on the other of losing our identity and of being submerged by the group. The Trinity offers us this new vocabulary of belonging. It celebrates the uniqueness of each individual person, but within a community of belonging together.'

The small group structures that are such a striking

feature of renewed churches can give the individual Christian just such an opportunity to belong. And in renewed Christian parishes and communities we see an emerging pattern in which each renewed individual contributes his or her particular gift in a greater sharing of the life, work and ministry of the Church among all the members. The lay person in renewal is entering into the kind of spiritual life and is receiving gifts of ministry that in the past have been the province of the solo professional. Lay people living ordinary lives are not only being drawn to affective prayer, but are being given gifts of contemplation that were supposed to be only for the enclosed religious. (See Chapter 3.) Lay people are beginning to exercise a variety of priestly, 'spiritual' ministries alongside their traditional contribution in administration. As a result an endless variety (one might say a confusion) of eldership schemes, shared ministry schemes, lay pastoral assistants, and so on, proliferates. One of the most striking characteristics of renewal is what the Report *The Charismatic Movement in the Church of England* called 'the coming-to-life of the laity'.

This is the direction in which the Church is moving, rather than where it has arrived. Meanwhile everywhere there is a ferment going on among lay people who are seeking, searching, wanting something more; and there is a management crisis among clergy as they endeavour to cope both with the changes that are taking place, and with the change in their own role, from being a one-man-band to being conductor of an orchestra, with various intermediate stages. So the style of priestly ministry that has been with us since at least the thirteenth century, when our present parish system took its form, is withering on the vine, and a new style of leadership is painfully emerging. The unicellular parish structure that has also been with us since medieval times is under severe strain, while in some parishes which are experiencing renewal a new multi-cellular structure is already superseding it. New forms of liturgy and new insights into corporate worship are changing the familiar patterns of Anglican life, to the deep distress of some, and to the delight of others. Quietly, and with pain and struggle, a gentle revolution is taking place. Pastoral problems and a great need for leadership with the ability to manage change are emerging in its wake.

A striking feature of the Church today is the deep spiritual hunger of many lay people. They are looking for a deeper spiritual life and for the fellowship of those who are travelling the same path. To meet this need there has been a burgeoning of retreats and conferences to which they can go to find the teaching and support that they cannot always find in their own parish, where a 'lowest common denominator' in spirituality can sometimes prevail. The hunger for spirituality, the drive towards a deeper experience of God, the shift from discursive methods of prayer to contemplation, the resurgence of English mysticism—all of these contrast sharply with the dry academic approach of the institutional Church which has created large patches of desert through which many people are still struggling. The springs of living water that are emerging in spiritual renewal are needed to irrigate the whole Church. The 'Jesus in the heart' way of prayer (see Chapter 3), current in the meditation movement and in the charismatic movement, is restoring a balance which the whole Church needs to recapture if it is to address the spiritual hunger of our age and restore wholeness to individuals and to the institution.

Balance is difficult to achieve. It is not so easy to integrate head and heart, spirituality and theology, prayer and action. But without such integration the pendulum can swing the other way to an unreal 'super-spirituality'. 'All bubble and froth and no theology', 'soulish and dreamy, not quite with it', 'a retreat into private holiness', are three descriptions of such a lack of integration. Donald Allchin gave us a timely warning in the 1970s that the irrational must not be allowed to become anti-rational and to sink into the sands of sectarianism (*The Kingdom of Love and Knowledge*). The Anglican *via media* has traditionally sought a combination of deep piety and sound learning. Those clergy who not only have this combination, but also possess the much rarer ability to communicate it, are much in demand for counselling and teaching, conferences, spiritual direction and retreats. Lay people need enabling to go deeper in the life of prayer, to articulate their faith and to apply it in their everyday situation.

However several religious who give retreats or talks on prayer commented how much easier it is to talk to lay people than clergy about the spiritual life. Some clergy are discouraged in the whole field of spirituality. There are more activists than quietists among them—'Can't dream about when there is all this work to be done'. Others are seeking to redress what they feel is an imbalance in their training, and to go further in the life of prayer. Theological college courses concentrate on establishing a basic theological literacy but academic demands tend to take over and spirituality can get squeezed out into the margins. George Carey, who taught at two other theological colleges before his present appointment as Principal of Trinity College, Bristol, said to me, 'The academic approach after a while becomes very sterile, you are looking at theology as if it were an object, instead of responding to God as a person to adore, to worship.' He went through a period which he described as a 'desert of the soul' until it dawned on him that if he relied only on the academic he would soon be 'dead' or useless. Christianity had become just an intellectual affair. 'I looked at, I

7

discussed, I studied, I reflected upon it, rather than being aware of it as something that studies me as well. Spirituality is a process of change rather than a form of knowledge. I dream of theological training which puts spiritual formation first, and information second.'

While the ministerial training given at national and diocesan level has often concentrated on the academic, there has been a considerable growth in the number of extra-parochial communities serving the needs of clergy and laity on this spiritual quest. The traditional religious communities have an important part to play, but there has also been a mushrooming of modern communities, groups, retreat houses and conference centres. Many of these are in the mainstream of Spiritual Renewal and are making a vigorous contribution to it.

Canon Ivor Smith-Cameron, the Southwark diocesan missioner, was asked by his bishop to describe to him the state of the Church and the life of mission in his diocese. He replied in a paper which describes the *Five Faces of the Church*. The first face is those members of the Christian community who have by their faithfulness, loyalty and perseverance maintained the life of the Church over the years. Their numbers have gradually declined. The average age of those on the electoral roll in the diocese is 59 years; so this is a withering face. The second is the laity among whom the ferment which I have described is taking place. They are busy going on courses, and there is a burgeoning of lay discipleship in this group all round the diocese. They represent the new life. The third and fourth faces are extra-parochial communities and task groups which are also full of new life. Some of these communities have their face turned inwards towards the Church and are servicing its members, but others are concerned with the needs of the wider society outside. Many people are finding an expression of

Christian service through the life and work of these communities or groups. The fifth face is a large number of men and women who are right on the fringe of the Church. They are seekers. They do not wish to sign on any dotted line, or to commit themselves totally to any of the mainstream Churches, but they too are pilgrims on a spiritual journey. In his conclusions to the paper, Ivor Smith-Cameron suggests that the Church, and certainly the Bishop, ought to be equally concerned with all these faces, and to encourage a greater variety of ways of relating to them in the diocese.

In practice national and diocesan Church structures are mostly concerned with the first and second faces. These two faces represent the two strongest polarities within parish life: the traditionalists who want stability and resist change, and who (if they are looking for renewal at all) are looking for a more lively form of their own tradition; and the reformers for whom things can't move fast enough, and who are getting involved in the modern renewal movements. These two groups are pulling in different directions, and sometimes the parish is being split in order to manage the needs of both. It is often said that renewal is divisive. In fact the division is often there already, but is highlighted by any move towards change. If the parish does not move to accommodate those who want change, they are likely to drift away in despair. Many have gone off into the rapidly growing House Church movement, convinced that the Church of England is never really going to be renewed. On the other hand, moving too quickly, or sometimes simply moving at all, will marginalise or alienate the traditional group. Some parishes have split the congregation deliberately in order to try to contain this problem.

But when renewal comes to an individual, to a group, to a parish, or to a conference meeting, it brings with it

9

a rebirth of faith and hope. Everything seems possible again. 'It gives me confidence that the Spirit of God really can renew the face of the earth', said one woman to me of Cursillo. A lack of dynamic hope has seeped into the Church. Many people pray expecting the answer no; their whole attitude is negative, they do not expect anything to happen, they just carry on and do their best. Spiritual renewal brings a resurgence of hope, love and trust. As the Churches' Commission on International Affairs commented in a report to the World Council of Churches, 'Christian faith ... gives us the capacity to act hopefully in hopeless situations'. Whether the ground of that hope is 'because the risen Christ goes before us', or 'because Jesus is coming to meet us', the experience of renewal raises the level of expectation of what God will do. I had to queue for an hour and a half to get into a conference on healing, which was being supported by people from all over the country. What was striking about the people in the queue was the hope on their faces. They were full of hope and joy and eagerness, a looking forward to what God was going to do next.

But coming down starry-eyed from the 'mountain-top' experience to the situation below, they encounter a very mixed reaction. Incomprehension—'Father has had this lovely experience, but what are we to do about it?' (Anglo-Catholic parishioner). Conflict—'The Spirit comes, and he's so radical, the structures can't take it' (Charismatic). Hostility—'We were impossibly excited, we wanted to be Christians seven days a week, not just on Sundays. We were so enthusiastic we got on everybody's nerves' (Anglican who joined the House Church movement). Questioning—'Is the radicalism a breakthrough or a blind alley?' (layman). Or downright rejection—'Fifth-rate jiggery-pokery' (Peter Mullen on the Charismatic Movement). Martin Israel, speaking of the retreat movement, said, 'You can get people on to a "spiritual high" in a weekend, but they have got to come back to the same old problems on Monday morning. The problems have to be transfigured, not avoided.' For many people, clergy and lay, the biggest problem they encounter at the foot of the mountain, waiting to be transfigured, is the Church itself. 'How is one to live in this awful body, the Church, without being shackled by it?' is the problem as articulated to me by a priest in Anglo-Catholic Renewal.

But while some people are repelled by renewal, others are attracted. It pulls in people from a wide area, and a renewed parish is often an eclectic one. Students in particular seem to have a nose for renewal, and they appear as soon as it starts to happen. Indeed, a striking feature of renewed parishes is the number of young people that they attract. Repelled by the deadness and by the traditional mode of so many of our churches, they are hungry for spirituality, and zoom in eagerly at the first signs of new life. The emphasis on experiencing God here and now that one finds in renewal may be significant here. As Brother Roger of Taizé says in his book *Living Today for God*[1]:

> In claiming the right to live as they think best, the younger generations show their determination to fulfil their human possibilities. History and all that the past offers are viewed with suspicion; what counts is direct, here-and-now experience, living fully in the present rather than becoming a part of any pattern or system. Perhaps this sense of urgency springs from an awareness of living on borrowed time, with the past poised on the verge of destruction and perhaps a whole civilisation with it.
>
> Christians must see clearly where their responsibilities lie in this situation, remembering that the Gospel too professes a form of existentialism, a call to live to the full

---

[1] Fuller details of sources quoted are given at the end of each chapter.

11

each present day, given by God. Joy disappears for the Christian anxious about the future. There is a kind of folly in the Gospel that runs counter to the human longing for security.

'What worries me', said a clergyman, 'is the shift from justification by works in the pre-Reformation Church, and justification by faith in the post-Reformation Church, to justification by sensation and experience in the present Church.' Certainly there is a new emphasis on experience, and this chimes in at a very deep level with the counter-culture of our age. Experience raises the level of faith and whets our appetite to know more of God. The driving force behind spiritual renewal is a hunger for relationship with God. This longing for God is stimulated by seeing him at work. Julian of Norwich leaps across six centuries to us, when she says, in her *Revelations of Divine Love*:

> It was he whom I saw and yet sought. For here we are so blind and foolish that we never seek God until he, of his goodness, shows himself to us. It is when we do see something of him by his grace that we are stirred by that same grace to seek him, and with earnest longing to see still more of his blessedness ... So I saw him and sought him, I had him and wanted him. It seems to me that this is, and should be, the experience of us all.

Alongside the quest for experience in today's spiritual renewal there is a shift from private to corporate religion, from 'me meeting God' to 'God with us', experiencing afresh or for the first time what it really means to be the body of Christ. What has been emerging in the Church through spiritual and liturgical renewal has been the corporate experience of God expressed in *koinonia*. 'God with us' is at the core of the renewal—the corporate experience of the immanence of God, expressed in living worship and grasped in our relationship to our neighbour. 'What is emerging', in the words of Graham Cray, vicar of St Michael-le-

Belfrey, York, 'is a Church in which relationships are paramount, not hierarchy, where leadership means being keeper of the vision and where authority is seen as a gift which is perceived through a servant spirit.' Carlo Carretto, the Roman Catholic hermit, who speaks with the voice of renewal, says, 'The great, official, solemn Church, replete with ceremony, with visible power, with numbers, no longer impresses. Today's people, knowing the anguish of loneliness, want a Church made of friendship, of genuine contacts, of mutual interchange of little things. But more than anything else, a Church that feeds them with the Word, a Church that works with them by physically taking them by the hand, a Church whose face is like that of the Church of Luke, of Mark, of John, a Church that is just starting . . . that smells of beginnings. No one wants to switch Churches if their own Church offers them what they seek and thirst for, truth, love, friendship, personal relationships.'

In some of the renewed churches that I visited I experienced a quality of *koinonia* that I have previously met only in a Christian community that was living together. It was not just friendliness but the fruit of a deep commitment to Christ and to each other. As one woman put it, 'Jesus gives us this love that we have for each other; we wouldn't have the strength otherwise.' In the eclectic parishes, where establishing community is more difficult, a concerted effort is being made to bring people together in groups. Even in the more conservative parishes there is a strong drive towards fellowship. In one that I visited the fragrant smell of freshly ground coffee brewing at one end of the church, redolent of fellowship, vied with the smell of incense, symbolic of worship, at the other end.

As this corporate experience is being built up, a corporate witness, far more effective than any individual testimony, is being made to the presence of God

13

and his Kingdom among the congregation or community. The sense of the presence of God and of the *koinonia* among the congregation is very attractive to many incipient Christians. They come looking to God to meet their needs and to fulfil their humanity. They stay to worship when they catch a glimpse of God at work in the body of Christ. 'You cannot teach worship to someone who has not got a sense of the living God', says Archbishop Anthony Bloom in his book *Living Prayer*. But this sense can be caught in a prayerful, worshipping community. Renewal starts with individuals committing their lives in penitence and faith to God, but it happens in the context of community. 'I find God here in a way I cannot anywhere else' said one woman to me of a renewed church. Another said, 'The first time I came here I felt that I had met Jesus.' She became a Christian and persuaded her husband to come along. He was put off by her enthusiasm at first, but ended up by being converted too. A striking feature of renewed churches is the presence of numbers of new Christians in the congregation.

So even without great efforts at formal evangelism and mission the renewed church can grow numerically, as it attracts and holds new members. But a strong drive to bring people in can put a strain on the parochial structure. As David Wasdell's work has shown, the unicellular parish structure is only adequate for a congregation of around two hundred, of whom on average sixty-five are likely to be in church at any one service on Sunday. As numbers rise above this figure the quality of relationships goes into decline, and the numbers go into decline too, unless the congregation is broken down into smaller pastoral groups where people can make relationships more easily. If this is done, the groups will support a larger number, so that multi-celled parishes in renewal will continue to grow until they start to burst at the seams in terms of buildings and parish boundaries. This brings problems in our present parochial system. When the congregation becomes too big for its buildings and then for its parish boundaries, where is it to grow to? This is a new problem for us in this country. Here, in contrast to Africa and South America, we are not used to seeing healthy churches multiplying and dividing, and planting new churches, apart from exceptional circumstances such as in a new housing estate. But alongside the dying churches that are struggling to keep going, there are now churches vibrant with new life, looking to plant new churches, yet bottled up by our parochial boundaries. It is very difficult telling people in eclectic parishes which have experienced a renewed church life to go back into other churches which have not been renewed. As one bishop put it in the words of the old song, 'How're you going to keep 'em down on the farm, now that they've seen Parée?'—or its church equivalent in terms of renewed worship, new styles of ministry and new understandings of corporateness. There are signs that one or two dioceses are beginning to allow the planting of daughter churches, or to allow a renewed church to revive a neighbouring church that was about to become redundant, for example; but there is also strong resistance from other clergy in the deanery to allowing a new church to be planted within 'their' territory.

The old church is dying, and a new one is coming to birth. As one diocesan missioner put it, 'What we need in the situation are good midwives'. But, as a religious said, 'What side are we on? I want to be with the dying life, not with the living death'. In the Church today we are inextricably entangled with both, if we are involved at all, and both are painful.

The Church has increasingly become a museum rather than God's house, a cemetery full of sepulchres rather than a living body. Like relations coming back to

15

remember their loved ones, and like the faithful women in the Gospel who returned to the sepulchre to venerate the body of the 'dead' Jesus Christ, faithful Christians pay respect to the past but forget the promise of new life. Increasingly the tradition has become heavy and lifeless, more and more difficult to hand on to the next generation, and the crisis which hit the Church in the 1960s (when the mismatch between the tradition and present-day reality became so great that it had to be faced) is still with us. But it was then, at a time when influential theologians were pronouncing that 'God' was dead, and when the traditional perceptions and structures seemed to have reached the end of the road, that the spirituality which had been simmering underground in the 1950s began to come to the surface within the Church, in the form of spiritual renewal. From a fresh encounter with the living God flowed not only new perceptions and attitudes, but also new relationships and new structures. 'The feudal age of Christianity is coming to a close', says Carlo Carretto, '. . . We are at the end of an age and . . . a new age is suddenly beginning . . . Think of yourself as building for a new tomorrow, rather than defending a past already old and moth-eaten.' (*I sought, I Found, My Experience of God and the Church*.) Spiritual renewal is the dynamic which is enabling this rebuilding to happen, and, in a world that has turned pagan, the Church in renewal is being rebuilt for mission. It is surely no accident that while this death and resurrection is taking place in the Church, society at large is going through a similar kind of travail. We are experiencing the dying of the industrial heartland and the birth of the post-industrial age. We have passed the end of Renaissance man, and are now in the post-Enlightenment age. I will leave the sociologists to explore the relationship further. Let me simply say here that, though there are obvious parallels, the

Church, I believe, is not just a mirror of our society, and the renewal not simply a baptism of the counter-culture. My research leads me to believe that what is happening through renewal in the Church is significant not just for the Church but also for wider society. As the Dublin Agreed Statement (1984) of the Anglican-Orthodox dialogue says:

> The Holy Spirit praying in us heals and renews us at the very centre of our being, that is to say, in our hearts. The healing character of the grace of the Holy Trinity in the life of the individual believer and of the Church has important implications for the whole life of contemporary society.

In other words, it is not just the individual believer that is being healed, but the very heart of our society. Some would go further and say that the Church is (or should be) a demonstration model of the Kingdom, that it is, in a prefiguring form, the new society. In so far as it is failing to be that, it is failing in its vocation and showing the need for renewal. The inward structures, the very heart of the Church, have become so depleted that a time of inner restoration and of putting one's house in order may be necessary before the new life can begin to make an impact outside. Others feel that to wait until the Church is right would be to wait for ever. They want to get on with the renewal of society now, and have moved out into the more radical groups at the fringe of the Church's structure. But for both the task has been to learn how to relate to one another within new structures, with new ways of belonging and a fresh understanding of authority.

Renewal is a worldwide and ecumenical phenomenon. This study looks only at the Church of England, but it is important from the outset to see it as a reflection of something that is permeating all the mainline Churches in the world. A recent study of four other Churches in the Anglican Communion showed a development parallel to the lay ferment and management crisis in the Church of England. That research demonstrated an emerging tension between the 'lay awakening', in small group movements and the charismatic movement, and the traditional clergy-administered church in which clergy and bishops are experiencing severe stress. The tension between the two groups seems to be increasing, and according to the researcher, Dr Brian Hall of the University of Santa Clara, California, this dynamic needs to be consciously managed. A critical position seems to have been reached in the history of the worldwide Church in which the leadership has a key role to play, but so far has had great difficulty in adjusting to it.

'There are big shifts in society generally', a clergyman told me; 'there is a shift of power, loss of mystique to the clergy ... the Church's structures are teetering on a knife edge—the future is exciting!'

DETAILS OF SOURCES QUOTED

Living Today for God: Brother Roger of Taizé, Mowbray, Oxford, 1980.

'Towards a Trinitarian Renewal of the Church': Tom Smail, published in *Theology of Renewal* magazine, No. 25.

'The Five Faces of the Church': Ivor Smith-Cameron (unpublished).

I Sought, I Found, My Experience of God and the Church: Carlo Carretto. Darton, Longman and Todd, London, 1984.

Long-Term Planning and the Church: David Wasdell. Urban Church Project.

Dublin Agreed Statement (1984) of the Anglican/Orthodox dialogue. SPCK, London.

Living Prayer: Archbishop Anthony Bloom. Darton, Longman and Todd, London, 1966.

Revelations of Divine Love: Julian of Norwich. Penguin, Harmondsworth, 1966.

The Kingdom of Love and Knowledge: A. M. Allchin. Darton, Longman and Todd, London, 1982.

Chapter 2

THE CHALLENGE OF CRISIS

Spiritual renewal implies a restoration of something that is in decay. Something that has been lost has been given back to us; something that we have fallen away from has been put back into our lives. The renewal movements have sought to restore an emphasis, to bring back an element that has gone missing in the life of the Church. Each in its own way taps the root of our vocation to find a spiritual spring to water our particular patch of desert, a source of power to meet the challenge which faces us.

The challenge of crisis begins the process. Whether spiritual renewal is personal or corporate, the ongoing experiences of everyday Christian life or the landmark experience of the contemporary renewal movements, it goes through three identifiable stages. First of all comes *crisis*, a challenge (either external or internal) that brings us up short, which does not allow us to continue along our present path without response and adjustment. Secondly, a *search* for the right response, and for the resources to carry it out, an attempt to break through on a spiritual level. Thirdly, the *breakthrough itself*, bringing new insights, fresh resources, new purpose and direction. I found all three stages of the process within the Church today, personal and

21

corporate, in exterior circumstances and at an interior level. At an interior level the crisis may be a feeling of emptiness, a sense that there is something missing, an experience of the absence of God; the old concepts of God seem unreal. Christopher Bryant, in his book *The River Within*, said, 'The experience of the absence of God is an unsought initiation into the negative way of approaching God ... psychic energy is being drawn away from conscious beliefs and ideas towards a knowledge of the heart ... God speaking through the deep centre.' Anthony de Mello in *Sadhana* (p. 53) says that unless our way of praying goes from the mind to the heart it will dry up. 'Many clergy and religious think that prayer is a matter of thinking, and that is their downfall.' For some this spiritual crisis is experienced as a drying-up of the prayer life, an aridity which makes intellectual prayer impossible, leading to complaints of an inability to pray. Others are experiencing a dark night, a sense of the inability to see, think or feel anything. However, far from going away, God is coming closer, but is out of focus. They are entering the Cloud of Unknowing, the symbol of the transcendent God, who cannot be grasped by the reasoning intelligence, but is perceived intuitively at an unconscious level. Others feel a sense of inner division and frustration; there is an awakening to symptoms that tell them that something is wrong, and lead them to search for a cure. They may not be sinning consciously against the light, but there may be serious underlying spiritual blocks to be dealt with, or they may simply have gone too far in one particular direction, and need to change course. We don't hear about that old-fashioned thing called conscience any more, but Father Bryant said:

> God is there within the self as an inner guide; when we infringe the law of our inner self, symptoms begin to appear.
>
> ... So it may well be that an individual's first experience of

THE CHALLENGE OF CRISIS

God is of his judgement. God's judgement is however always merciful and is in fact persuading him
to change the attitude which is causing inner division
and frustration. (*The River Within*: Christopher Bryant,
SSJE).

The crisis can also be an external one. Many people
today are starved inwardly, while being continually
pressured to put all their strength into exterior tasks,
and they find it hard to sustain the demands made on
them. When a personal or family crisis comes, the
resources are not there to meet it. Our society is under
increasing strain and tension. Scientific progress has
landed us in the nuclear nightmare, materialistic
progress has proved a hollow failure, with many people
facing unemployment and redundancy. The Welfare
State, the caring society idealistically and hopefully
launched after the last war, is crumbling under the
pressure now being put on it, particularly in the large
cities. The family unit is increasingly giving way under
the strains of modern secular society. I found all these
problems mirrored in the congregations of the parishes
I visited, and in the renewal movements.

A lay evangelist said to me 'When I go knocking on
doors, I know there is a problem behind every one, but
the biggest problem, and the most common one is
loneliness. I tell them, "Jesus is your friend".' In this
isolation of loneliness, other problems of life can seem
overwhelming. John Gunstone, in his book *A People for
His Praise* (p. 138), says:

> Young people and adults who come forward for baptism
> often do so with a heritage of emotional or spiritual
> problems. Indeed, the act of conversion may be associated
> with a desire to overcome personal difficulties in their
> lives—drug addiction, immorality, an unhappy marriage
> and so on. Preparation for baptism will then involve
> counselling and inner healing. In the early Church
> preparation for baptism included ministries of this kind to

rescue catechumens from the evil influence of the pagan society in which they lived. The services, known as 'scrutinies', were held during the week before the baptisms at Easter, and were designed to deliver the candidates from the power of the devil (the solemn renunciation of the devil and all his works, still a feature of most baptismal liturgies, is a relic of these services). Modern society's influence is no less evil ... It is naive in the extreme to assume that an individual's personal problems will be solved when he confesses his faith in Jesus Christ as His Lord and Saviour and asks to be baptised. He will probably need much support from the pastor and the congregation before the victory of the cross is manifested in his life.

The Church that looks outward from itself to care for the community can find itself sucked into an apparently bottomless pit of need which is beyond its resources to meet. 'We are overwhelmed with ministering to people with problems', said the vicar of a large city parish.

Another parish in a big city was also facing similar difficulties. 'We don't think we have grown marvellously', said its vicar, 'because we put ourselves in the light of the need that abounds all around us. We are appalled at how little we are achieving, because we realise that there are thousands outside who are helpless and hopeless. The Social Services have in many respects broken down in our area ... We know of a tremendous amount of need outside that we need to grow large enough to help, but the larger you get, the more of those sort of needs you get, because every one of our people that is helped has ten or a dozen people who look to our team for resource and help ... The other problem that one faces in society is that people who are in employment are doing three people's jobs, and so are working too hard in any case, and these are normally the people who are our resource people with ability to minister. What we are now doing is to train up the next generation of caring people from those who have suffered, and are just beginning to get stabilised and healed, virtually to replace our over-busy experienced people, who have caught their own maximum workload over the years. If we become inward-looking again, what will happen to us is what has happened to other churches, and what did happen to our church in a previous day. We've got to be looking out into the wider community.'

For clergy the crisis often manifests itself in what is happening, or not happening, in the parish. Some parishes are on a survival course and find it hard to maintain themselves, let alone undertake the task of mission. Clergy can find themselves trapped into a declining situation, working harder and harder to sustain a shrinking status quo. The renewal movements are full of testimonies from clergy of the 'my goings had well-nigh slipped' variety. 'Before renewal, I had tried everything, and had come to the conclusion that the Gospel didn't work', said John Gunstone to me. Lawrence Hoyle of Anglican Renewal Ministries was a converted Evangelical, but he had not been told about the Holy Spirit. He had picked up the impression that once you were converted, you worked hard at it; you didn't dare admit that it wasn't working properly, or else you might be zapped around the head with a zipped-up Bible, or told that you weren't saying your prayers properly, or having your quiet time properly! He tried this muscular hard-at-work Christianity for a time, but cooled off. He became more and more frustrated, and after several years of going round parishes doing his tricks and finding them not working, he began to think that he was in the wrong job, and that he shouldn't have been ordained.

The experience of spiritual renewal within a parish can intensify the crisis many clergy feel about their authority and their role. As lay people come to life in renewal, the whole relationship between clergy and

25

laity needs to be re-negotiated. One parish I visited had been involved in renewal for sixteen years, and lay participation was mature and advanced. A young couple, a curate and deaconess straight from theological college, had just come, and though I was told at the theological colleges I visited that students were being prepared for shared ministry, these two were totally taken aback by the situation they faced. Lay people were leading the Bible Study groups, they were leading and arranging the worship, and the newcomers were told where they could fit in. They expected automatically to be put on the eldership group that ran the parish, but were told by the vicar that they would have to wait a bit and win their spurs first. 'Why have we been ordained?' they were saying, 'What have we been to theological college for three years for? All the things that we have been trained to do are being done by lay people'. The vicar's answer was, 'You have felt called to ordination, and the Church has affirmed your vocation. But you need to die to the role you thought you had, and discover within this community what in fact it is that God is calling you to'.

The crisis may be a corporate one. A traditional religious community that I visited was in decline. They had a high proportion of elderly religious who needed care, and could spend their entire time looking after them and after their buildings, but this conflicted with their felt vocation to mission. They were committed to caring for their elderly, but were questioning everything else they were doing, questioning its authenticity and its purpose, asking, 'What are we here for, what are we about?' They saw their crisis as opportunity. They felt that they were being called into a much more costly brokenness, that they had erred into rigidity even in the best expression of their life, and were in danger of losing their humanity. They were going into an uncertain future, but becoming more real, more human, more listening. God was calling them to listen to one another and to recognise the unique richness that they possessed through a diversity of gifts and calling. Some of them were being called to put down deeper roots into God, and to engage in spiritual battle. For the community as a whole there was a shapeless agenda of waiting and praying as they attempted to think through their task creatively and to aim more accurately at the goal of their existence.

Their situation mirrors the condition of many parts of the Church of England at present. The crisis of faith and of order that hit the Church of England in the sixties is still reverberating around it. In company with other Churches it found itself in a post-Christendom situation, marginalised within society and finding it difficult to sustain itself and its mission. Some feel that the crisis is less acute than it was, but it is still painful. 'Younger clergy have never known the secure Church that I was ordained into before it was shattered in the sixties; they don't believe it when I tell them', said an older clergyman. Instead of society being Christianised, some feel that the Church has become secularised. This inability to Christianise the environment and to make Christians of the next generation is a crisis of mission that provokes some basic questions. Cardinal Suenens in *Ecumenism and the Charismatic Renewal* (p. 5a) says:

> Without resorting to statistics or sociology we have merely to ask ourselves 'Are we Christians truly Christianised?'
>
> ... In the early days of Christianity, adults were truly evangelised, but subsequently we entered an era when baptism was conferred on infants as soon as they were born. Society became nominally Christian, sociologically Christian. Therefore Christianisation was regarded as something already achieved, sustained by the social context, and passed on from generation to generation.

It is clear that this process is no longer being carried out adequately, in a milieu which is no longer Christian.

The Church needs to be renewed for mission in a secular age. But it is encumbered with unbending structures that are not geared to mission. They assume a captive audience, already initiated and conversant with the Christian way of life. Many parish churches are impenetrable for outsiders. No amount of exhortation or pressure can motivate them into mission—the spiritual energy is not there.

The Three Days, a commentary on the talks given at the Cursillo weekend, gives in its outline of the 'Christian Community' talk the following headings which describe the ideal situation we ought to be in:

A. Why are you here?
  (1) God called. Yes.
  (2) But it is through the response of a Christian community that you are here.

B. What motivates the community to reach out to share God's love?
  (1) We have found grace (the love of God).
  (2) We have lived the Eucharist.
  (3) We have found friendship with each other.
  (4) We feel a sense of mission.

But for how many parishes today would the honest reality be:

C. (1) We are unfulfilled.
  (2) We are going through the motions without much hope or expectation.
  (3) We are lonely.
  (4) We don't feel like mission.

Imposed efforts towards mission have short-term results but leave the parish in the long-term precisely as it was before. It is positively resistant to newcomers, who soon fall away. There is a need for new life, new motivation and new structures.

Prebendary John Gladwin, Secretary of the General Synod Board for Social Responsibility, in an interview I had with him, used the word *crisis* in relation to our age, our society, and to the Church.

> Crisis is a hackneyed word, but I use it deliberately. 'Crisis' is saying that there is a profound period of change going on which means that there are choices to be made. They are going to be painful. They can be destructive, or they can lead us to a more hopeful place for the Church and in society. There is no avoiding the agenda of painful adaptation; if we don't face it we are faced with irrelevance and a continued decline into a fossilised society. Are we going to be a museum piece? Or a place where we are participating in the working out of the meaning of God's Kingdom for the future, where we are discovering something fresh? There is a judgement on our past, there were good things, but an incompleteness is beginning to surface. We must move beyond the rigidities of our present system. We are called to move, develop, change and grow within a structure, in solidarity with the Kingdom of God, going with the grace of God rather than towards his judgement. We need institutions to give us support, resources, structure. But the social order is creaking. Our institutions are not assisting us, and the Church is no different in this regard. That the Church has got it all right and the world has got it all wrong won't do. The Church is a mirror-image of our society, but it carries within it a living faith, and has a living Lord who can break and has broken the fetters that bind people and societies. We need models of relationships which work, and of structures which work.

One of the most deeply-felt crises in all the Churches has been their inability to pass on their tradition to the next generation. A clergyman in Anglo-Catholic Renewal felt that some people within the Church have become anarchistic; they are so frustrated and exasper-

29

ated with the institutional forms that they more or less kick over all traces. He felt that there was misunderstanding of what the tradition was about, that it had represented itself badly. 'A lot of problems spring from our models of what the Church is, which are inadequate models for the present situation. We are still wedded to the parish structure, still wedded to the threefold ministry.'

I found a great deal of dissatisfaction among those committed to Anglo-Catholic Renewal. They have been tenaciously holding the line against an erosion of values and belief, but this has led to a sense of beleaguerment, while the battlegrounds have changed. There was criticism amongst them of the negativeness, the defensiveness, the rallying to the party flag only when there is a threat, rather than a grasping of the opportunities for a positive and outgoing renewal. 'What is being renewed', asked the Bishop of Leicester at Loughborough 1983, 'the Catholic Movement, or the Church of England?'

Anglican Renewal Ministries find that there is impatience and frustration everywhere. Two kinds of people come to them to unload. The first are casualties of the traditional Church who have complied with the lowest common denominator of commitment which the Church seems to require, but who find that if there is a real crisis there are not the resources to meet it. The other casualties are casualties of the Charismatic Renewal, individuals who enter Renewal by going to big meetings, blowing their top and getting so enthusiastic that when they go back to their own Church, full of enthusiasm, they put people off by their simplistic way; so, finding it all too difficult, they come to Anglican Renewal Ministries to be fed and encouraged. Many people have moved out of renewal or into the House Churches from a sense of frustration, particularly frustration with the vicar, who is very often the cork in the bottle. They have been given a vision and experience of what things could be like, but it is hard to be patient, to wait and pray for new life in the parish. Anglican Renewal Ministries try to encourage them to love people rather than try to change them. 'It's as if God was saying "You love them, I'll change them", but that is the yucky bit that people find it hard to tune into. They get frustrated and irritated with the traditionalists who seem to put up barriers. But behind the barriers people are very threatened.'

The tension between the lay awakening, the renewal movements and the traditional establishment has to be understood against this background of discontent with the status quo of Church life. Many people seeking renewal today have had a negative experience of Church life—it has not given them what they were searching for. An experience of God in renewal reinforces their faith, but any further experience of the Church that is negative can take them back to their first impressions with disastrous results. Memories are very selective; good memories tend to be very good (we forget the snags) and bad memories are very bad (we forget the mitigating circumstances). The inner message that such people are carrying around is that God is good, but the Church is bad, that God is real, but the Church is unbelieving and worldly, that the leadership in the Church must be at fault; they are responsible for the situation, thus their authority, their validity, is questioned. We are walking in the light, but the darkness is out there in the Church. The Church of England is like the shadow side of ourselves; can God, can we accept it? Who will take the blame for the unsatisfactory situation we find ourselves in? Is the Church 'them', or 'us'?

'Outbursts of enthusiasm are usually a sign of a breakdown in Church order', says Hans Küng. And the crisis question that the Charismatic Movement is facing

31

is one for the whole Church—is the Church of England going to be renewed? The Charismatic Movement has split between those who are staying in and who are involved in the renewal of the existing Church, and those who have left, saying that it is not God's will to renew the traditional denominations, and that they are either dying or dead. As I went round parishes I was told of increasing hostility between the Restorationists in the House Churches, who believe that in the House Church God is restoring a more New Testament form of Church, and the denominational Churches, particularly the Church of England. In one parish I visited, a group of their young people had been told by a House Church group that the Holy Spirit had left the Church of England, and that they should come out from among them, which they did. I was told that at a big gathering of the House Churches that takes place annually, those present who were ex-Anglicans were asked to put up their hands; when they did so, they were asked to repent of their Anglicanism. This hostility is not universal. I was also told of more than one instance of a House Church fellowship supporting Anglican ordinands through their training with financial help, prayer and moral support. But a letter from Gerald Coates, one of the leaders of the House Churches, to *Renewal* magazine, said:

> ... It is about time the Church of England, among others, asked why institutional Christianity has lost over 200,000 members in the last five years, and the so-called House Church Movement has gained 180,000.

But some believe that for the institutional Church as a whole the crisis is still not deep enough to bring her up short, to bring about the necessary change of direction, the *metanoia* required for renewal. These are some of the comments and quotations made to me:

> The Church is still too comfortable and too wealthy to

change. Things have to be desperate before we turn to God. We have to come to the end of our resources first. Renewal in the Church will come when we let go of our possessions.

Is there renewal in the Church of England? It seems to be in an awful mess. The church where I was married is faced with redundancy—£90,000 to mend the roof or else.

We are in the grip of principalities and powers.

Days of Fasting, Repentance and Intercession for the Church of England. Opportunities to do something positive about:
   1. The theological and moral confusion in the Church of England.
   2. The failure of the Church to evangelize the nation.
   3. The need for the Holy Spirit to renew the life of the Church.
(Advertisement in *Anglicans for Renewal* magazine)

When everything is crumbling, then one is facing reality. (St Augustine)

The challenge of crisis must be strong enough to bring about a change of direction, but not so strong as to reduce us to despair. For spiritual renewal to take place there also needs to be a confidence that God has an answer to the problems, that he has put within the situation the resources for the task, that there is in him a way forward that we can find. And though there is a crisis, there is also in the Church of England a new confidence in God. There is a searching going on, a searching to break through on the spiritual level, and there are areas of breakthrough where spiritual renewal is taking place, where new life and new structures are emerging, which are encouraging people to believe that the unsolved problems can be tackled, that God is in control of the situation, that the dry bones can live.

DETAILS OF SOURCES QUOTED

The River Within: Father Christopher Bryant SSJE. Darton, Longman and Todd, London, 1978.

Sadhana, A Way to God: Anthony de Mello SJ, Anad Press, India, 1978.

A People for His Praise: John Gunstone. Hodder and Stoughton, London, 1984.

Ecumenism and the Charismatic Renewal: Cardinal Suenens. Darton, Longman and Todd, London.

The Three Days, A General Commentary on the Lay Talks of the Cursillo Weekend (p. 253): National Ultreya Publications, P.O. Box 210226, Dallas, Texas, 75211, USA.

Letter from Gerald Coates, *Renewal* magazine No. 117, June/July 1985 (p. 39).

Advertisement from *Anglicans for Renewal* magazine No. 22, Summer 1985 (p. 31).

Chapter 3

THE SEARCH

The master was asked, 'What is spirituality?'

He said 'Spirituality is that which succeeds in bringing one to inner transformation'.

'But if I apply the traditional methods handed down by the masters, is that not spirituality?'

'It is not spirituality if it does not perform its function for you. A blanket is no longer a blanket if it does not keep you warm'.

'So spirituality does change?'

'People change, and needs change. So what was spirituality once is spirituality no more. What generally goes under the name of spirituality is merely the record of past methods'.

('True Spirituality' from *The Song of the Bird*: Anthony de Mello SJ. Copyright 1982 by Anthony de Mello, SJ, Reprinted by permission of Doubleday & Company, Inc.)

'There must be more to life, but what is it?' The woman in the pew behind me had articulated the unspoken question that is motivating people all over the country to search restlessly in the age-old quest for meaning and for fulfilment. This woman had been a Christian all her life; she had read her Bible, prayed, come to church, but there was something missing. Like the rich young man in the Gospels she was asking 'What do I yet lack?'

At a prayer workshop I visited a similar questioning was going on.

When I talk to men of my age (56), I find they are angry.

And if you talk to the women, you find they are depressed.

Depression is repressed anger.

What are people angry about?

We are unfulfilled—there must be more than this.

...But how can one know the unknowable?

I still have doubts, but there is something there, in the silence.

Wherever I looked, at points of spiritual growth and renewal, a journey inwards was going on: people coming to faith, people with faith coming into a new experience of God, those with experience of God longing to go deeper, being drawn into silence and contemplation, and among the contemplatives a call for some of them to the hermit life, to be totally alone with God. I found this inward movement in all kinds of situations, and in different sectors of our society. It is not just a middle-class phenomenon, although middle-class 'booky' people tend to dominate and to be more articulate and more active in their search, though they are not always quite sure what they are looking for. The inward movement is taking place outside, as well as inside, the churches.

As in the sixties, our counter-culture today is full of people who are searching, trying to understand the nature of reality through drugs, transcendental meditation and the occult. To them the Church can seem the last place to come to find help in their journey. It seems too occupied with its own agenda, answering questions that they have not asked. Christopher Bryant said to me, 'A powerful surge of human spirit is seeking blindly to regain contact with the divine, and diffusing a mood of dissatisfaction with things as they are. While theolo-

gians are labouring like their eighteenth-century predecessors to demonstrate the reasonableness of Christian faith, a growing public is taking an interest in
astrology, spiritualism and black magic.'

But it is easier than it has been at any time in the last
forty years to talk about God to ordinary people, and to
get a response, as the 'Mission England' teams found.
'Something in the communal psyche must be shifting
worldwide', says a diocesan missioner. 'The social
structures are crumbling—there is a fear of what is
happening in the world, and no trust in humanist
solutions, people are looking for other foundations,
and turning towards God.' The response to 'Mission
England' far exceeded the dreams that its organisers
had for it, but the problems came when the attempt was
made to integrate enquirers with the life of their local
church, in spite of the care that had been taken to train
Church groups in the nurture of the newcomers. The
cultural chasm that divides churchgoers from the rest
of society is now so wide that communication across the
frontier of the community of faith is fraught with
difficulty. Newcomers complained of the theological
talk that they were given in some churches instead of
spiritual nourishment. It is spirituality that they are
after, and a spirituality that is relevant for today.
Further evidence of this trend comes from the Association for Promoting Retreats, which is having to
respond to people who will not darken the door of a
church, but will go to a retreat, and ask for spiritual
direction.

People's needs and perceptions are both more
simple and basic, but also more sophisticated than the
Church generally allows for. Enquirers want to know,
quite simply, whether Christianity is real, and whether
it works. We live in an age of anxiety; many people
today are overstrained and tense, they need to be
helped to relax physically and mentally into the love of

God and to learn not just to believe in his existence, but to trust him. Jung complained before the war that theologians were too intent on proving the existence of God, instead of helping people to experience him. The renewal movements have an experiential element which helps to meet this need. And when people's basic needs are met, they are capable of much deeper and broader development than is commonly supposed or catered for. The creativity and potential that they have is there in embryo, waiting to be developed and tapped, but frustration can lead to bitterness and alienation. There are tremendous opportunities for the Church at the moment, opportunities that become problems if they are not grasped.

In an age of instant coffee, people often expect an instant spirituality. Some people think they have arrived, when they have only just embarked on a lifetime's journey, bordered by eternity. The evangelical message of the salvation accomplished for us by Christ is read as 'You've got it all now', instead of 'You're accepted, and now you can get on with it'. Renewed churches often attract new Christians, or Christians who have been 'switched on' for the first time, and have to rear them and 'bring them on'. One church in the Charismatic renewal is known in its diocese as 'the Nursery'. The clergyman of another parish engaged in renewal told me 'I have an adolescent church, with an adolescent spirituality that mistakes excitement for life'. There is a sense in which we are all beginners in the spiritual life. A nun who had been a religious for fifty years, when shown an article called 'Prayer for Beginners', said, 'Ah, that is good for me also, one can always begin'. The question is, are we growing, are we developing? It is impossible to give a single answer to that question, because the situation is so variable. Certainly the Church leadership that I talked to was very conscious of the need to move people on spiritually, but in many areas the population is so physically mobile that churches are continually having to start again and build up from scratch, as new people come in and others leave. In those areas which are more settled and where renewal has been going on over a long period, one can see the maturation process at work; in the Church of England generally the investment in developing spirituality at all levels is far too low, and consequently the potential of its members is not fully employed.

There are many who need to be lifted by spiritual renewal from 'a Christian life that is mediocre and individualistic with limited horizons' (Edward Bonin, founder of the Cursillo movement). Others who have experienced renewal exhibit a youthful arrogance and immaturity, as well as a youthful ardour and enthusiasm. Spiritual experience is no yardstick of maturity. Some are finding that their own Church has gone dry, and are looking beyond their parish boundaries, across the barriers of churchmanship, and beyond their own denomination to find an appropriate spirituality. A whole stream within the Church is on the move.

But, as Martin Thornton says, 'Individual spirituality is not just a private luxury, but the essential life of the Church and the source of its mission'. Even the sixties radicals who were at one time scornful of any kind of withdrawal into a holy huddle are seeing the necessity for deeper resources, for the Church to be a place of support and encouragement where they can find the spiritual strength to tackle the radical agenda without running out of steam. An Anglo-Catholic commented on the Evangelical clergy he met in his deanery, 'The Evangelicals are getting even more churchy than we are'. But there is also a resistance against treating the Church as a petrol station, as a place where you get 'topped-up' spiritually, and also against its becoming merely an ambulance-station on the fringe of society, picking up its casualties. Those on the move are looking for something more dynamic than that. They are seeking a creative encounter with the reality of God, and the reality of themselves, which will enable them to find the way forward. They are exploring unknown territory, which some find exciting, and others daunting. Some are hanging back, because the way forward isn't clear.

> In the country of the Spirit
> there is a place
> of transition.
>
> There my tent is pitched;
> the glorious immensity
> of the night sky
> obscured by canvas walls.
>
> To retrace my steps
> is to lose my soul,
> to move forward
> seems impossible;
> no clear route
> is to be found
> on this country's map.
>
> Only gracious invitations
> from seasoned explorers
> and signs of contradiction
> which tease heart and mind
> encourage me to strike camp.

(*Outside the Camp* by Sister Gillian Mary SSC)

We can only understand within a frame of reference or a mental boundary; but in looking at God we are faced with a Being who is beyond our mental framework, who is closer to us than breathing, but who slips through, under and out of our mental boxes. When we try to encounter God, we enter into a darkness, a cloud of unknowing. The seasoned travellers can give us good advice and have given us an example, but they cannot make our journey for us. We must set out in faith, like Abraham, not knowing where we are going.

This sense of entering into unknown and uncharted territory leads to a preoccupation with guidance. How are you to know whether you are on course or not? By the fruits perhaps, but they take time to appear. People are looking for signposts to help them to find their way, for touchstones to interpret what is happening to them. The way in which we perceive reality is changing, our way of praying is changing. In order to understand the search for a spirituality for today that is taking place, it is helpful to look at the signposts and touchstones that are being used, to discover which parts of the tradition are coming alive for us in the present, and how they integrate with new insights into the nature of how things are.

One charismatic I talked to carried in his wallet a kind of spiritual compass for finding the way forward to new understandings and new action. It was designed by Segundo, a Latin American theologian, and was based on a modern management tool (See p. 42).

The Bible is still the principal touchstone for spirituality, particularly for those who are involved in Renewal. It is being studied with more care by those who have traditionally rejected the insights of modern biblical criticism, and with greater confidence by those who have accepted those insights. (The symbols are more powerful than the intellectual difficulties.)

Christian discipleship has in the past flowed from the picture of Jesus that the Gospels give us. How does modern discipleship deal with what biblical criticism has to say about cultural packaging and the way in which the Gospels were written? The current mood of confidence is reflected by John Austin Baker, Bishop of Salisbury, who wrote in a recent article:

41

I have come to three conclusions as a result of many years of academic study. First, both the narratives and the sayings in the Gospels are much more accurately preserved and historically reliable than many would have us believe (and this goes even for the miracle stories which cause many Christians so much embarrassment today). Secondly, a study of the setting of the material is necessary but when carried out it reveals not something which time has rendered irrelevant but a deeper relevance transcending cultural change. Thirdly, where the community tradition which handed down the material to the Evangelists or the Evangelists themselves have seemingly commented on, rearranged or modified the words and stories, we need to remember that they were themselves members of the Church, devoted to Jesus, and illuminated by his Spirit. Careful and fearless study of the Gospels can only enrich our devotion and prayer, and lead to new inspiration for the following of Jesus today. We learn and ponder and meditate and adore not just to satisfy curiosity or arouse emotions but to know what God requires of us. ('Radical Discipleship': John Austin Baker, Bishop of Salisbury. *Grassroots* magazine, September/October 1985)

Several of the clergy I talked to emphasised the necessity to study the whole Bible in order to achieve a balanced spirituality. One deplored the modern tendency to pick out the bright bits of the Psalms rather than the penitential bits—'Bless the Lord, O my soul', rather than 'Be merciful to me, O Lord'. There was a tension here that he felt had not been resolved. Indeed, complaints about a general lack of penitence came from clergy in all parts of the Church. In the Anglo-Catholic Renewal, some feel that the Anglo-Catholic movement achieved most of its basic aims by the 1950s, with the exception of the sacrament of penance, which has not met with general acceptance. Even in circles which use the sacrament I heard complaints that people were not using it correctly, that they were not confessing things of real significance. What people do seem to need and want to do is to pour out their weaknesses, doubts, fears, things which are not technically sin, as well as things that are, and to be reassured of God's love, power and forgiveness in their weakness. This can be done in an informal way with the help of clergy, but often happens in lay pastoral groups or counselling sessions. This seems to resolve the tension between people's need to be reassured that God loves them and accepts them as they are, and their need to deal with the painful agenda of things in their lives that need to change, and with which they find it difficult to cope. Many people today in our loveless age are wounded and suffer from feelings of inferiority. They have no proper self-love, because they have not been loved. The Biblical writers assume self-love—we are told to love our neighbour as ourself—but for many people today it takes much love and reassurance, not just talked about but embodied and expressed, from the Christian community before they can believe that God loves and accepts them as they are. The following chorus attempts to deal with the problem.

> Let us open up ourselves to one another, without fear of being hurt or turned away; For we need to confess our weaknesses, To be covered by our brother's love, To be real and learn our true identity.
> (No. 81 in *Songs of Fellowship*; © 1978 Thank You Music, P.O. Box 75, Eastbourne, BN23 6NW).

Over the last twenty years Evangelical practice and lifestyle have broadened out, become less distinctive and culturally richer. Many Evangelicals are becoming more radical as a result of re-reading their Bible and addressing what it says about social justice. An Evangelical Charismatic Radical said to me, 'Just as I need to wonder how I had read the Bible but hadn't taken in the bits about the Holy Spirit, now I am wondering how it was that I missed before all the references to social justice.' The movement of Charismatics into the radical field has meant that social activists among Evangelicals have become less hostile to Charismatics than they were in the past, and that there is collaboration and convergence. The radical and subversive aspects of spirituality have been explored; reflection, spirituality and worship have assumed greater importance among Radicals than in the past, and are seen as part of maintaining the sharpness of radical involvement. An unresolved issue is the understanding of the Church: how much should one be looking to the Church as an alternative community that bears testimony in the world as to what the world should be about, and how much should the Church be a community of support to people scattered and diffused in secular society? The coming-together of Charismatic Renewal and social action has tended to go with the former model. A Charismatic Radical emphasised to me that the balance between spirituality and social action comes about through teaching the whole Bible, asking the following questions:-

What is the nature of God?
What is his intention for the world?
How does that impinge on me?
What ought I to be doing in response to it?

This is close to the approach of the Ignatian exercises, which are used as the basis of some retreats. They use Biblical texts to explore the nature of God, and to draw out the filiation of the Christian to Christ so that one asks oneself, 'What am I doing for Christ, and what ought I to be doing?'

Modern English Radicalism has been criticised as being either impulsive, romantic reaction, or pragmatic and philosophically weak. I encountered some radical work with a real cutting edge (see Chapter 6), but it is comparatively rare. The contemporary Renewal Movements in England have yet to produce their Wilberforce or Lord Shaftesbury, though there is a confident expectation among Radicals that such leaders will appear. Much of the effective work being done by leading Radicals is happening among groups working right at the fringes of the Church's structure, and their thinking has not yet become integrated into the mainstream of Church life.

Since the beginning of the Charismatic Movement, those within it have looked particularly to the Acts of the Apostles and to the Pauline Epistles for affirmation and understanding of the Charismatic experience and the function of the charismata in the body of Christ. But a change of emphasis is taking place. 'People think that the Charismatic Movement is all about the gifts of the Spirit, but what it is really about is the Lordship of Christ', says Lawrence Hoyle of Anglican Renewal Ministries. That emphasis was certainly there at their big conference at Swanwick in 1985. But as the Spirit points us to the Son, the Son points us to the Father, and the trend in the whole Church of the eighties to focus on the Trinity is also mirrored in the Renewal Movements. Some think that the Charismatic Movement as such is over. I saw no evidence of this, but rather signs that it is growing (though more slowly than in the seventies), consolidating, and moving into a new phase, in which it is converging with other groupings, such as the Radicals on one hand, and the Meditation Movement on the other. It is also splitting between the Renewalists and the Restorationists, between those who are staying within the denominations, working and praying for their renewal, and those who are leaving and joining the rapidly growing House Church Movement. Among student groups the Free Church/Anglican rift has deepened, but the Charismatic/non-Charismatic divide is breaking down. Those who are not Charismatics have re-examined their assumptions and adopted a more conciliating position, while Charismatics are looking to recover good relations and are fraternising with others. But there is a resistance to the House Church Movement which has some similarity to the churches of the Brethren, and which at one time appeared to be taking over the Christian Unions.

At the present time some people are re-reading with new eyes the accounts of the healing ministry of Jesus, and particularly the injunction in Luke 9. 2 to preach the Kingdom of God and to heal the sick. Though the revival of a healing ministry within the Church has its origins back in the beginning of this century, it is only now becoming more integrated into the centre of Church life. This is happening widely but particularly so in circles that are experiencing Charismatic Renewal, where it has received impetus from the 'Third Wave' campaign led by John Wimber and his team from the Vineyard Fellowship in the United States. They have been encouraging Churches to take on board the healing ministry not only as an ongoing piece of work among their fellowship, but also as a means to evangelism, a demonstration of the Kingdom of God at work. This emphasis draws its inspiration from a confidence that in the accounts of the healing miracles of Jesus and the Apostles portrayed in the New Testament we see an aspect of the Christian life which should be a permanent feature of the life of the Church. An ordinand who wants to engage in the ministry of healing told me that he felt that the average Anglican does not accept miracles. He believes that God is doing miracles all the time. He has seen people healed and his wife has been completely healed of depression. 'So many people in the parishes are more dead than alive. I am interested in healing the whole person, and bringing the whole person to life'.

I found evidence that some physical healing is indeed taking place, but even more evidence of inner healing. I talked to people who had received physical healing which was medically vouched for, and to those who had received inner healing, in particular healing of painful memories which were a block to wholeness. I also talked to those who had not received healing, whose expectations had been raised only to be dashed again; and who were finding it hard to go on in faith. Both those giving the ministry and those receiving it tend to blame themselves for lack of faith or spirituality when nothing appears to happen, but nobody can really say why healing sometimes occurs and sometimes does not. We are confronted by a mystery here; we are caught in a tension between 'now' and 'not yet'. One clergyman with a long-standing healing ministry was sharply critical of healing as a means of evangelism. 'God is sovereign and does not do deals'. The situation in most churches that are offering healing ministry was summed up by one curate—'There have been some wonderful healings and answers to prayer, but also failures, and times when we have felt out of our depth'.

The Bible is also sometimes being held as a bulwark against change, particularly in the field of the relationship between men and women. It is quoted in some Evangelical circles as a reason for not allowing women to participate in leadership, even in parishes where much of the natural leadership is coming from women. In one Charismatic parish I visited women had been allowed to become elders, but only at the end of a ten-year struggle, in which those who wanted a male-dominated hierarchy split off into the House Church, where the roles of men and women tend to be governed by rigidly patriarchal attitudes. This was counter to the general trend of Church life, which inclines towards a greater participation of women in the life and ministry of the Church. One response to the Questionnaire which I sent to the dioceses commented that the number of women coming forward for lay ministry had increased threefold in the last five years. But the significance of a more fundamental shift, allowing the whole community to show more of the caring, feeling, intuiting side of human nature which has traditionally been held for society by women, seems to go unremarked. A 'thaw' in the personality, leading to the emergence of these values is a striking feature of renewal.

The Future Breaking In

It's more than that, you know.

More than deciding
who opens the door
who chairs the committee
who waxes the floor.

Or allowing the woman to speak
in a sacred place.

The vision
is just stirring in the shell
and requires a tearing
a breaking up of pieces
a release from the past.

The vision
is Woman
turning into a woman
and Man
turning into a man
who'd rather care than compete
who spend some time listening
who writes 'sister' and 'brother'
instead of 'Dear Sir'.

Who give up their life for each other
feeding
healing
touching
forgetting that one was called great
and one was called nothing—
people free to need each other.

In the unity
of One Spirit.

49

Where each person is the Gift
and The Giver
and no one goes without a name.

(Greta Schuum)

Another major development that has been taking
place in the last twenty years has not received enough
attention. There has been a fundamental shift in the
way in which Christians are praying. What is happening
is that the centre of our praying is moving from the
head to the heart. The three touchstones that are being
used to interpret this journey are Jungian psychology,
the fourteenth-century English mystics, and Orthodox
spirituality. They all speak of God as dwelling within the
centre of the personality, waiting to be found.

> Jung's concept of the self, as he was well aware, accords
> closely with the Christian mystical tradition, especially as
> we meet it in the fourteenth and two following centuries
> ... To become aware of God, the individual must enter
> into the darkness within him, the unexplored hinterland
> of the personality ... The old masters insist that the
> experience of God is no mere intellectual knowledge. It is
> a heart knowledge, in which emotion and instinct,
> intuition and the irrational, body as well as soul must
> participate. It is in line with this ancient wisdom that the
> spiritual guides of the Eastern Orthodox Churches
> describe true prayer as holding the mind in the heart.
> (*Jung and the Christian Way*: Christopher Bryant SSJE, p.
> 48)

Val Nobbs, a member of the Post Green Community,
wrote for their *Grassroots* magazine an account of how
she had found understanding of what had happened in
her spiritual life through a study of Orthodoxy. In
renewal she found God in her heart and in the hearts of
her companions in the community. She had been
brought up to believe that one found God by denying
one's humanity, but now she found her humanity being
affirmed. It was '... in fact not an obstacle but a crucial

50

key; to know and love and accept myself was to move towards God. To understand this truth, and to live believing it set me free to enjoy who God had created me to be'.

Alongside a new awareness of the immanence of God she also became conscious of his transcendence.

> To seek God is to go from the known to the unknown, to move from the light of partial knowledge to a greater knowledge the darkness of unknowing. God is not so much the object of our knowledge as the cause of our wonder.

The Orthodox view is that God cannot be grasped by the mind. If he could be grasped, he would not be God. But though God is beyond what we can say or think, he can be experienced in our hearts and in the community of the faithful, and in creation.

> I realised, with a great sense of relief, that my idea of God had been too small. I had been taught to define him in terms of what I could know and understand until he seemed little more than a puffed-up version of myself . . . To discover Orthodoxy was at last to make sense of my experience. I realised, with great relief, that others thought as I did. There was a West, but also an East. I had found a place to anchor, a tradition reaching back to early Church history, of which I was a part and to which I belonged.
>
> ('West meets East': Val Nobbs. *Grassroots* magazine, July/ August 1984).

I found that clergy religious and lay people from all parts of the Church, including those who have no contact with the contemplative tradition, responded positively to the concept of 'Jesus in the heart'. Some Evangelicals are encountering Anglo-Catholic spirituality, and some Charismatics the Meditation Movement, as they seek an understanding of this development, as they find themselves being drawn into silence and affective prayer. The Neo-Platonic dualism that sifted out the spiritual from the material is giving way to a more integrated view of the nature of our humanity in which God is the core. The Orthodox would say that we in the West have been on the wrong track since the time of Aquinas, when the idea was accepted that human rationality was the only part of our human nature not to take part in the Fall, and was therefore safe and to be trusted. This caused a split in the Western mind, from which flowed a rapid development of rational thinking and of science, philosophy and academic theology; but behind a facade of lofty ideals the area of the unconscious mind was largely ignored, and lagged behind, unhealed and unredeemed, from which arose the collective sickness of society. An Indian Christian, Sadhur Singh, expressed this in a parable of a stone that he had taken from a Himalayan stream, which, although it had been lying in water for hundreds of years, was dry as a bone inside when he cracked it open. He likened it to Western civilisation, which though it has been lying in the mainstream of Christianity for hundreds of years, has not let it penetrate to its heart. Mystical experience was to be found in the Church, but it was thought of as exotic and special or downright suspect, and not integrated into the mainstream of Christian theology or structure. Western theology emphasised the transcendence, the otherness of God, to such an extent that he became 'Deus ex machina', the God of the gaps, receding into the distance until he seemed to have disappeared altogether. But modern understanding has moved on, leaving this perspective stranded. A recognition of the spiritual dimension within creation, approached by faith, is paralleled in modern science.

Jung was acutely aware of the collective sickness and the collective evil of the world in which he lived. The material and spiritual havoc that we have experienced this century come from this repressed barbarism, the ugly contents of the unconscious mind. How can this be healed? Jung answers that the ugly contents of the unconscious must be brought to the surface where they can be dealt with. The way to do this, Jung recommended, was through Christian contemplation. But at the time in which Jung was writing, Christian contemplation was little known outside convents and monasteries, it was the preserve of the specialist, the professional. The result was that some spiritual searchers turned to the mysticism of Hinduism and Buddhism, to the Oriental methods of contemplation in order to find what they were looking for.

(*The Mirror Mind*: William Johnston, p. 145 ff).

'If only we had taught them Christian contemplation', a spiritual director said, 'they wouldn't have needed to look to Eastern methods'. Many Christians were and are very uneasy about looking to other faiths for the way forward, for this lays itself open to the charge of syncretism. There may be superficial similarities between Christianity and Eastern religions, but there are fundamental differences in outlook and standpoint also. Jung himself was uneasy about what he saw as a flight into the Oriental. He saw the dangers of using Oriental methods without Oriental faith, and of jettisoning the foundations of our own religion, tradition and culture. 'The way is indeed through Christ', says Martin Israel. 'The trouble with using techniques is that you can get beyond the problems without solving them. The whole thing can become a kind of spiritual drug. The whole person, problems and all, must be transfigured by the spirituality.'

The situation has moved considerably during the last twenty years. Our whole way of praying has become more affective and contemplative. Martin Thornton says:

Contemplation used to be a frightening word, and it is one which comprehends a vast range of prayer and experience. But if its root meaning indicates an integrated, intuitive, experiential approach to prayer instead of a

discursive, intellectual one, then it has become the norm ... Emphasis on personal integration, on potentiality rather than substantive qualities, on total experience instead of pure cognition has led thousands of the modern faithful to simple non-discursive prayer; the encounter of the whole man with the whole Christ. Such prayer has to be called contemplative, although there is nothing very special or advanced about it.
(*Spiritual Direction*: Martin Thornton.)

The Meditation Movement in the Church is the place where contemplative spirituality is encountering the modern renewal movements and the spirituality of our age. The Association for Promoting Retreats is faced with an increasing demand from people, many on the fringe or entirely outside the Church, for basic spiritual guidance and the provision of a retreat experience. Retreat houses are dealing with clergy and lay people who come from a busy working life and who have not had the opportunity to devote their lives to interior spiritual development. The traditional retreat is not a group experience, and today the emphasis is shifting from the preached retreat to individually guided retreats. People are wanting to go deeper and to have spiritual direction. Retreats attract people from a variety of churchmanship, and provide the kind of encouragement and motivation among lay people that leads them into lay ministry. But there is a shortage of clergy who are trained for this work.

In response to this movement, the religious have opened their doors and have become a resource for those who are looking for guidance, although monastic spirituality and discipline is necessarily different from the spirituality of those in an active secular occupation, and needs translating. But from them has come a timely reminder that spiritual life and growth are not found in the exotic or extraordinary. They are concealed but accessible to all in the ordinary events of daily life.

The path of spiritual progress is essentially ordinary. It is not outside the path of normality, but in it. It is simply a case of natural growth in what God intends for us all, requiring the immediate contact with him which is the listening responsiveness of contemplative prayer ... The normal development of prayer takes root in the context of silence and listening, and flowers in the action of reconciliation in the world, the apostolate of prayer. (*Encountering the Depths*: Mother Mary Clare SLG).

From the religious life there comes also a much-needed reminder of the importance of manual work. Manual work is despised in our society; those who do it are on the bottom of our pecking order, but the monastic movement has from the earliest times recognised the spiritual significance of work with the hands, and many people pray best with their hands. One vicar I talked to had noticed a spiritual quickening among the congregation which emanated from a group who were cleaning up the church. The men up on the ladders cleaning out the gutters and the women on their knees polishing the floor were praying as they worked.

At a retreat house I met a woman who was being drawn to contemplation, and who had felt that God was calling her to ministry. She had gone to her vicar and asked whether she could go on the diocesan lay ministry scheme, but was told that she wasn't academic enough to do it—it meant writing lots of essays and she wouldn't be able to manage that. And he couldn't see how she could have any kind of ministry in the Church without doing a course of that kind. 'I felt really put down and angry—I'm not stupid.' She went to her spiritual director and asked if she was on the right track or not. He reassured her, and it became clear gradually that she was being called to a ministry of intercession. Now as she cares in her work for old people, 'working with my hands leaves my mind free to pray for them', and as she cleans her church and prays for its renewal, she is sharing Christ's ministry of intercession with the Father, (which in the spiritual realm is no doubt more effective than writing essays!).

Many who have considered the insights of Eastern religions have returned to their own roots, but with a deeper faith and trust in their own tradition and Christian understanding. I found that people in the Meditation Movement were using physical relaxation, posture and self-awareness exercises from Yoga and Zen, but their meditation is generally Christ-centred, and draws on the experience of Christian mystical tradition. The spirituality of the fourteenth-century English mystics is popular, particularly that of Julian of Norwich, and of the unknown author of *The Cloud of Unknowing*. Julian is now a religious best-seller; Julian meetings have sprung up all over the country in recent years, and, at an informed level in the Church, interest in her work is growing, though more so in America than in England. She is not simply a devotional writer who has comforting things to say to us about God's love and mercy, but an astonishingly modern theologian who has important things to say about the nature of God. She speaks from an age which was overshadowed by the Black Death and from a society which (like ours) was under strain and tension, in an age of transition caused by the break-up of feudal society. Her reassuring message comes from this background, and from a vision of the cross, rather than of heaven. Her vision of God is of his infinite compassion and love; he regards us with pity, not with blame. He rejoices in the sacrifice he made for us; she sees no anger in him. He is our Mother as well as our Father, and he redeems all of us; there is no division between the spiritual and material. She does not see the spiritual life as a ladder; rather we are all like children trying to walk, tumbling over, and being raised up by our Father/Mother, God. Her vision of Jesus, enthroned, reigning within the soul, corresponds with modern spiritual experience and emphasis. He is not just an external authority; to be reconciled to him is to be reconciled to our true self, the ground of our being, and the law of our own nature created by him.

Mystical theology of this kind is rare both in Catholicism and Protestantism, but, as Donald Allchin says, the destruction of the man-made idol, the God of Western theism, has opened the way to a rediscovery of the living God who reveals himself as he did to Abraham, Isaac and Jacob, not as a concept, or an object of human knowledge, but as a mysterious Person, the Other, with whom we have a creative encounter at the heart of our human journey. He is being experienced afresh as the God of the Old Testament, who speaks to his people through his prophetic word and through events, to warn and to encourage. And he is being experienced as the God of the New Testament, who loves us and reaches out to meet our need and to reconcile us to himself, but also as a God who is troubling and difficult, who leads us, like Peter, where we do not wish to go.

The work that Jung saw as needing to be done, the bringing into consciousness of those parts of the unconscious, both personal and collective, that need healing, is now going on in the Church; but is frequently misunderstood. The purgative work of the Holy Spirit which sorts out all the things that block the way to wholeness—our faults, fears, errors, weakness, painful memories and that old-fashioned thing called sin—by bringing them up to the surface where they can be dealt with, can be misunderstood or wrongly handled without right teaching and spiritual direction. A few people have gone right off the rails as a result of a lack of experienced spiritual direction, while others have been needlessly distressed because they do not understand what is happening to them. Some of the deepest work that is being done at the moment is happening among the Church's leadership. At the end of a week-long conference on healing, John Wimber said, 'We have been ministering to you all week. You are full of fears, doubts and anxieties, and you are the leaders of the renewed churches'. Bishop Morris Maddocks says in his book *The Christian Healing Ministry* that the biggest need of the Church today is for a healed leadership, those who have received what he calls the 'Lord's deep-ray treatment', and who are then filled to become channels of healing to others, and to minister Christ's healing to the flock he has entrusted to them. So the healed Church becomes the Church of healing. A vicar's wife said to me, 'I am now able to thank God for everything that has happened in my life, and for the suffering of my childhood, because it gives me keys to other people's lives, and enables me to minister to them'.

And as individual sin and suffering are dealt with, the call comes to allow the suffering of the collective unconscious to surface, to identify with the deeper agony and wounds of the human race. A Charismatic group was taken aback and chastened to be told in a word of prophecy, 'You still have not yet got enough love to share the pain of your brothers and sisters in the Third World'. The work of contemplation in particular increases the willingness to suffer, to share the communal pain and suffering of mankind, and to offer repentance for the burden of communal sin.

At the national Partners-in-Mission Consultation, a Finnish monk, Father Ambrosius, one of the overseas partners, proposed the following diagnosis and treatment for the Church of England—'This Church needs a lot of praying and fasting and silence and solitude'. In the years since then, desert spirituality has grown within the Anglican Church, and a few within the contemplative communities are receiving a call to the hermit vocation. There are now some religious living in total solitude, like some of the early Celtic Saints, perched on the edge of the Atlantic coast. But an inner desert journey is also taking place, not only in the contemplative communities but also among clergy and lay people who are being drawn inwards to do deeply interior work. As Moltmann says:

> Earlier, mystics withdrew into the loneliness of the desert in order to fight with demons and to experience Christ's victory over them. It seems to me that today we need people who are prepared to enter into the inner wilderness of the soul and wander through the abysses of the self in order to fight with demons, and to experience Christ's victory there, or simply in order to make an inner space for living possible, and to open up a way of escape for other people through spiritual experience. And in our context this means wresting a positive meaning out of the loneliness, the silence, the inner emphasis, the suffering, the poverty, the spiritual dryness and the knowledge that knows nothing.
>
> (Jürgen Moltmann, *Experiences of God*, p. 61).

DETAILS OF SOURCES QUOTED

'True Spirituality' from *The Song of the Bird*: Anthony de Mello SJ. Image Books, New York, 1984.

Jung and the Christian Way: Father Christopher Bryant SSJE. Darton, Longman and Todd, London,1983.

'West Meets East': Val Nobbs. *Grassroots*, July/August 1984.

The Mirror Mind; Spirituality and Transformation: William Johnston SJ. Collins, London, 1983.

Spiritual Direction: Martin Thornton. SPCK, London, 1984.

Sadhana, A Way to God: Anthony de Mello SJ. Anad Press, India, 1978,

The Future Breaking In: Greta Schuum (unpublished).

Encountering the Depths: Mother Mary Clare SLG. Fairacres Press.

With Pity, Not With Blame: Robert Llewelyn. Darton, Longman and Todd.

The Kingdom of Love and Knowledge, The Encounter between Orthodoxy and the West: A.M. Allchin. Darton, Longman and Todd, London.

The Christian Healing Ministry: Morris Maddocks. SPCK, London, 1981.

Experiences of God: Jürgen Moltmann. SCM Press, London.

'Radical Discipleship': John Austin Baker. *Grassroots*, September/October 1985.

'Outside the Camp': Sister Gillian Mary SSC. *new fire*, Vol. VIII No. 62, Spring 1985.

Chapter 4

THE AWAKENING

A Modern Psalm

Blessed be God, Creator of All,
Magnify the name of God with praise and rejoicing,
For we cried out in thirst and longing,
With yearning hands we searched for God
With parched souls and dry hearts we prayed.
And God, who is love, has listened to our call,
For God has had compassion on our thirst,
And in love has given us to drink of the Son,
And in mercy has given us the water of eternal life.
Rejoice then greatly in God; Creator, Redeemer,
    Sustainer,
Celebrate with thanksgiving the greatness of God.

(Jan Fortune-Wood)

At the heart of spiritual renewal, after the crisis of emptiness, and the search for the missing element, comes a turning point, an awakening, a fresh encounter; a new sense or perhaps a fresh perception of the reality and presence of God. No matter what stage a person has reached in the spiritual life, there comes a point of breakthrough, a new awareness bringing fresh encouragement, energy, purpose, insight, lighting up the situation from inside.

In the 1958 Dale Lectures, the then General

Secretary of the World Council of Churches, W.A. Visser t'Hooft, summed up the elements that must be present in an individual or in a Christian community for spiritual renewal to take place:

> 'Be renewed' does not mean 'Get busy and find some different and better method of Christian action'. It means 'Expose yourself to the life-giving work of God. Pray that he brings the dry bones to life—Expect great things from him—And get ready to do what he commands'.
> (*The Renewal of the Church*: W.A. Visser t'Hooft).

It has been assumed that if people prayed, read their Bible, came to church, partook of the Sacraments, that they would therefore be open to God's action; but it becomes clear as one studies the renewal movements that there are all sorts of factors and variations which determine whether and to what extent this may (or may not) happen.

Renewal is God's action; but we have to be willing to submit to it, and this passive action is hard, because it goes against the grain of self. To surrender is to die to self-will. Two kinds of people find this particularly difficult in different ways; those with a strong ego, and those whose ego is not strong enough. The stronger our ego is the harder it is to surrender, but the stronger our love for God and our neighbour will be in the end. Our self-love has to be transformed into love for God and for our neighbour, for it is the passion that will sustain our spiritual life. The people who find it hardest to die and struggle most vigorously with God often make the best saints. On the other hand those who have a weak ego and who have little self-love and self-esteem find it difficult to make the necessary commitment. Until you possess yourself you cannot love God and your neighbour. Those who are in this position need to be strengthened and reassured before they can give themselves, believing that they will be accepted.

Many people in the spiritual life resemble the non-swimmer who is trying to learn to swim, but who is firmly keeping one foot on the bottom. It requires a degree of confidence and trust to let go, but this is something which we cannot work up, and into which it may take some time to grow.

> God is waiting to pour immense blessing on those who will rely firmly on him, but everywhere he is met with a corporate unbelief, mistrust or selfish anxiety, which create an atmosphere which stifles the personal faith of individuals ... God is present where he acts. He waits for us to open ourselves to him and will not force his way into our hearts.
> (*The River Within*: Christopher Bryant SSJE).

Christopher Bryant found that the people coming to his prayer workshops were tense and stressed. 'How can you express trust in God if your body is giving out danger signals, when the body is saying "Look out, beware, danger!" I go through a relaxation exercise with them first, getting them to be aware of the feelings in their body, and then become aware of God's presence.'

Renewal also requires a depth of repentance that gives us the willingness to change and be changed. Visser t'Hooft says, 'All great renewals in the history of the Church have been movements of repentance. This is inevitable because renewal presupposes a break with the old world. Repentance is turning from the old world to the new, from the past to the future, from the closed world to the open heaven, from egocentricity and church-centredness to God's Kingdom.' But to go from the known to the unknown requires a high degree of confidence and trust. Some people come to the Church precisely because they are insecure and are deeply threatened by any kind of change, internal or external.

Another difficulty is the inappropriateness of some of the spirituality that obtains in some parts of the

Church today—it is either too old-fashioned, or too cerebral. Some areas of the Church seem to be living in a time-capsule; the clock seems to have stopped around 1960, and they are finding it hard to relate and communicate the essence of their faith and devotion to people today, to their bitter disappointment. But the attempt to modernise through a more rationalist approach is equally out of tune with the mystical trend of many of today's seekers. The weakness of the tradition has led to a search for a return to the original dynamic of the Church, the direct encounter with God.

'There is no point in ministering to people if you can't bring them to God', a spiritual director said. But many people hang back through fear, mistrust or ignorance due to a failure in teaching, either at the initiation stage, or later on. Moving them on seems to take a more intensive effort than is generally available in the run-of-the-mill of Church life. The encouraging thing about studying contemporary renewal, however, is that it shows that most people who are willing to be Christians at all will open themselves more fully to God's action, given the proper teaching and fellowship of faith. Indeed some of the people I talked to were indignant that they had not been helped to do so before. 'I didn't know I could have Jesus in my life' said a laywoman who had been a Christian all her life. 'Nobody told me. When I knew, I wanted him'. 'I used to think that the Holy Spirit was just for Pentecostals', said a lifelong Christian whose search had brought her into the Charismatic Movement. 'Isn't it dreadful!'

Working with people in small groups over a residential weekend gives an opportunity for in-depth teaching, helps to break down barriers, and forms community. A small, loving, accepting group can help people to work through their difficulties in an atmosphere of faith and trust. The curate in the Charismatic Renewal who was taking his 'Enquirers' group away for the weekend, knowing that in an environment of prayer, teaching and fellowship the majority would experience the touch of God, is doing in principle, (though at a different level) what the Cursillo weekend aims to do with mature Christian leaders. The Charismatic will talk of the power of the Spirit, and the Cursillista will emphasise the grace of God, but they both aim to enable people to open themselves more fully to God and his action, so that they can be empowered and transformed. 'When you are mightily touched by God, you want to do things for God'. 'Let the Creator work directly with his creature, and the creature with his Lord', says St. Ignatius. But the emphasis in the Retreat Movement is shifting from preached retreats to individually-guided retreats, because people want dialogue and discussion as well as teaching, to enable them to be open to God. In contemplative groups there is a desire to share with others on the spiritual pilgrimage, to talk to each other, as well as to pray together.

As the level of faith and trust in the individual and in the group is raised, it is like the tide returning to a harbour; when the water level reaches the critical point, the boats are lifted from the mud, and they begin to float. When the level of faith and trust in God among the participants reaches the point where it becomes operative, breakthrough can occur. As Moltmann says in *The Open Church* (p. 44), 'The heart opens itself for reception'. He is talking here of Christian meditation and contemplation, and continues, '... What kind of knowledge do we gain through meditation? When we wish to know something with modern scientific method, we know in order to dominate or control, that is, we appropriate the object. In meditation exactly the reverse occurs. We do not appropriate Christ for our use, but we give ourselves over to Christ for his kingdom. We do not change him, but he changes us. We do not "grasp" him, but he grasps us.'

Hilary Wakeman (in an article in the *Tenth Anniversary* magazine of the Julian meetings) says, 'But because the practice of contemplative prayer is observably good for us, it is very tempting to let that become our reason for continuing with it. Groups that have not yet established themselves are particularly prone to an emphasis on meditation as combating stress and facilitating self-development. I don't deny that these are by-products and that they are good. But the ideal group puts the emphasis firmly on a different motivation, seeing contemplative prayer as a way of making ourselves more and more available to God and so bringing his marvellous kingdom a little more into being.'

If the characteristic of the recipient in renewal is of openness to God, the other characteristic of spiritual renewal is that it is an experience of the Holy Spirit at work. As one diocesan missioner said, 'It is difficult to say what renewal is charismatic and what is not, because all renewal is of the Holy Spirit, but not necessarily of the Charismatic Movement'. The Cursillo movement predates the Charismatic Movement by twenty years, and is not Charismatic in the usual sense of that word, but the Holy Spirit is invoked at the beginning of each session.

> All: Come Holy Spirit, fill the hearts of your faithful and kindle in us the fire of your love.
> Leader: Send forth your Spirit and we shall be created.
> All: And you shall renew the face of the earth.

The experience of renewal will vary from person to person, and the understanding of it will vary according to the context in which it is set, but there are identifiable characteristics which can be observed, though the understanding of what is occurring is of course a matter of interpretation. It may be a quiet, gentle realisation, or a more euphoric experience revolutionising a life or a ministry, or an encouragement or affirmation of what is already in progress. It may be a conversion-experience, or a bringing to life of an intellectual conversion. It may be a landmark experience, or an ongoing one, it may be an advance in the life of prayer and be an empowering for ministry and mission. Here are some examples which illustrate a range of personal renewal experiences, beginning with two contrasting ones from the Cursillo Movement:

> I imagined that in some mystical, magical way I would be changed so that everything would be clear-cut and I would be on a constant spiritual 'high'. By the final morning of Cursillo I felt desolate, as if Father Christmas had forgotten me. I had hoped during the whole weekend that something amazing would happen to me, but I felt just the same.
>
> I remember sitting in the Chapel feeling very empty, looking for something I could not find. A gentle realisation came to me in the message of Cursillo. I had been looking so hard for my faith, over-analysing each emotion, crushing it; I had simply been searching so hard that I had not noticed what was there all the time. Jesus had patiently waited at my side through all my clumsy, over-enthusiastic ways of trying to make him signify in my life the way I expected him to. He was still there when I stopped looking long enough to see.
> (From Cursillo magazine *The Fourth Day*, Issue No. 8, December 1984).
>
> As I look back in 'my' Cursillo, my mind is filled with a kaleidoscope of vivid images and impressions. Almost first among them is laughter and joy, and that is wonderful because we in the Church tend to be so serious. But there was also a deeply moving sense of the real presence of God moving and working among us. There was the hilarity of 'art work' and the marvellous stillness during Visitations. There was the form of 'free singing' and the depth and

67

breadth of worship. There was the happiness of completely relaxed friendship and fellowship within the Body of Christ, and the deeply moving and healing times of self-examination, confession and absolution ... Never in my 30 years as a conscious Christian, nor in my 21 years as a priest, have I ever experienced so visibly and unmistakably the personal and close love and grace of God and the wonder and joy of real Christian fellowship.

For me it was (and continues to be), a life-changing, faith-changing experience and yet at the same time I do not feel 'turned inside-out or upside-down'. What I do feel is immensely enriched and renewed. I have tried to describe to my family and friends what I feel, and the best I have been able to do is to come up with a series of pictures ... Cursillo, for me, was like emerging from a long cold winter into a marvellous spring; it was like going to a real live concert instead of listening to my 'tranny'; it was like changing our black-and-white for our first colour telly. In other words, a whole host of things which for me had been 'cool' and 'cerebral' and 'academic' and 'abstract' through this weekend have become warm and living and real and joyful ... But perhaps most importantly of all, in a very real sense I came away feeling that it was not actually about my pleasure and delight and enjoyment. What it is really about was the enrichment and renewal of my faith, vision and vocation so that I might shine with a new brightness as a lighthouse to guide others towards the love of God in Jesus. For me Cursillo is very much about 'what happens next', indeed about our Fourth Day. And because of the first three, I know the Fourth will be filled with the love and grace of God.

(Cursillo is a three-day course; the Fourth Day is the rest of one's life). (From Cursillo magazine *The Fourth Day*, Issue No. 9, March 1985).

The Charismatic Movement has a wealth of testimony to the effects of Charismatic Renewal. Canon David MacInnes says, 'The whole world becomes a sacrament alive with God's voice. God starts speaking to the recipient in a new way through creation, through

68

the Bible, through liturgy, through people. It over-comes the natural timidity and reticence of many English people, and makes them more confident and outgoing. It does not move them to left or right, but makes them more concerned about the situation in society, and brings them out politically.' A religious said that before renewal she experienced God as severe; she did not have great expectations, life was a grim struggle, more Cross than Resurrection. Charismatic Renewal made her realise that God was love. Another was dry, and in need of help—she felt warmth and love in the Charismatic group. Now her need is being met. She was empowered for ministry, given the courage to pray with other people. She is less exuberant than at first, but going on at a deeper level. Her spirituality is more incarnational and affirmative; she has broken through her shell and lost her fear of feelings. Material things have become sacramental, and her spirituality is more down-to-earth. An Anglican ordinand experienced the cleansing, healing power of the Spirit. 'I went into the garden, and asked God's help. Immediately I felt as if an excavator was digging out all the hatred, resentment and bitterness I had felt since my brother was killed; then it was as if there was a shower inside me, cleansing me and filling me with joy.'

Peter Peterken's 'personal Pentecost' was like a spring-cleaning, an opening of doors and windows of the soul to the breath of God that blew through everywhere blowing away cobwebs and dust, freeing him from fear and inner bondages. The whole world came alive with the presence of God, and his filial relationship with God became real for the first time. He found himself being able to open up to Christians of other traditions, encountering and being reconciled with those at the opposite end of the churchmanship spectrum. He found that the Charismatic experience deepened his interest in contemplative prayer and

69

meditation. He now takes retreats with a renewal emphasis. He finds that people need the Good News rather than counselling; he has been drawn into the healing ministry and is becoming involved in the struggles of his local community. The God he is encountering is consistent with the God of Scripture, who makes all things new, who does extraordinary things in ordinary lives, who is working in and through ordinary people in his Church today. He affirms the Charismatic experience, but says that it is not affecting the structures of the Church as it should. He finds that Charismatics tend either to despair of the structures being renewed, or wish to alter them in a way prejudicial to Catholic order.

The Radicals I talked to found that renewal was a continuing experience. 'I can do without what happens in church on Sunday' said an Industrial Missioner, 'but I can't do without worship, or Christian fellowship, and I am renewed as I speak to the people on the shop floor; God speaks to me through them'. 'I am renewed through worship', said another, 'it gives me my electric charge, but I think I get it because I am engaged in mission'. The experience of people in the Meditation Movement is of a more continuous renewal too. There are long periods when nothing dramatic appears to be happening, although the person becomes more whole and integrated; and there are times of breakthrough, when there is upheaval in the personality, inner blocks are dealt with, intuitions about the nature of God or action to be taken well up into the conscious mind, and there is spiritual struggle.

One of the functions of the Julian meetings is to give people an opportunity (not often available to them in the parish) to talk about their spiritual life. There is less emphasis on religious experience in traditional circles, and people from that background are more reticent about it, which is one of the reasons why most of the

70

evidence in this chapter comes from the renewal movements, even though the 'lay awakening' is taking place throughout the whole range of Church life. But those who had come out from more traditional parishes to retreat houses and conferences were more forthcoming, and from them I gathered that their experience was similar both to the landmark experiences of the renewal movements, and the ongoing growth of the Meditation Movement—times of breakthrough, following a long process of purgation or slow growth.

The characteristics of the work of the Holy Spirit are understood in traditional spirituality to be purgative (cleansing and healing), illuminative (through which a person is given intuitions and perceptions of the nature and reality of God), and unitive (the gradual leading of the person into a deeper union with God). But the classical idea that we progress in a linear fashion from purgation, through an illuminative stage, to union is under criticism today as an artificial construction. The 'spiritual-ladder' approach is being replaced by a perception that all three elements are present throughout our lives as a continuous feature of the Holy Spirit's work. A contemplative was described to me by a fellow clergyman as the most healed, the most whole person he knew; but this had been achieved by a lifetime spent in the work of contemplation, and of opening himself continually to the Holy Spirit. Nevertheless there are times of more intense struggle, which may occur at conversion but which are also a feature of renewal experiences in more mature Christians, and which represent a major upheaval in the personality. They have been interpreted by some psychologists as the regrouping of the personality around a higher centre.

Christopher Bryant's description of what can happen when an individual is opened up more fully to God's action brings a psychological interpretation to bear on the work of the Holy Spirit—the bringing up to the surface of faults which need correction, the healing of old wounds, the giving of fresh spiritual insights, and the drawing of the person towards God and the neighbour.

> There is an invasion of the conscious mind by spiritual insights and impressions, new expansion, and new energy. There is elation, inflation and loss of objectivity. The weakening of repression leads to a welling up of repressed anger, temptations, feelings of rage, hate or depression. The contact between the new spiritual energy and light with the emergence of the dark sides of the personality leads to a conflict and battle. The person needs spiritual direction; otherwise they can become discouraged or quietist. A group can help. The validity of the prayer experience can be tested by its fruit, but the fruit takes time to appear. Perseverance brings growth in freedom and peace, but the growth is uneven due to a gradual emergence of repressed elements—jealousy, greed and self-centredness. But the person belongs increasingly to God and to other people.
>
> ... Some need healing from old wounds as well as the building up of love and trust towards God and other people. This is what the Gospel promises to those who will open themselves to it. But instead of facing these dark things many Christians have been brought up to repress them under a facade of sweetness and light. Only when we face the darkness within us and open it up to God's healing power can we start to grow spiritually. Progress in the spiritual life is not just a question of whether people believe in the existence of God, and propositions about him, and wish to lead a good life, but whether they are willing to open up their psyche in trust to him and allow reconciliation and healing to take place at a very deep level.
>
> (*The River Within*: Christopher Bryant SSJE).

John Gunstone in his 'Impressionistic View of the Influence of the Charismatic Renewal in the Life of the

Church of England' (*Strange Gifts*, ed. Martin and Mullen, Blackwell) remarks that there is a saying in Charismatic circles that when someone is baptised in the Spirit they should be shut away for six months. Their exuberant enthusiasm can put other people off. And when individuals become more open to the Holy Spirit, they have to undergo a fuller personal cleansing and healing than before. Wise guidance and pastoral support are needed to see a person through this volatile period, until the personality settles down again after adjusting to the new situation.

Lack of teaching, lack of structure, and lack of a wider knowledge of spirituality sometimes lead to difficulties. Although what is known in the Charismatic Movement as 'Baptism in the Holy Spirit' (which is generally accompanied by speaking in tongues) is widespread throughout all the denominations and has perhaps received more publicity than any other spiritual experience this century, the understanding of it is still the cause of confusion and controversy. The confusion is compounded because people experience such 'baptism' at different stages in their spiritual development, and in different ways. Interpretations therefore vary, sometimes with bizarre results. At a Full Gospel Business Men's meeting, which is an inter-denominational Charismatic organisation dedicated to lay evangelism among business men, I listened to a testimony from an Anglican layman who seemed to be in a state of muddle about what happened to him. He knew that he had been truly converted as a young man and had given his life to Christ, but he had not developed or felt the touch of God in his life again until his experience of the 'baptism'. He therefore thought that his spiritual life had not been genuine—he seemed to regard his Anglican baptism as a kind of vaccination which had not taken, and which needed to be done again. He asked his Anglican vicar to 'rebaptise' him, but the vicar refused, pointing out that one does not need to be readmitted to the Church because God is working in one's life. The man did not accept this decision, and persuaded a Baptist minister to baptise him in the sea when he was away on holiday.

But in fact within the Baptist Church itself this difficulty can be even more acute. It is possible for Anglicans to argue that the 'Baptism of the Holy Spirit' is a further experience of the Spirit which has been given because we have not yet entered into the fullness of what we were given at baptism when we were babies, or because we were not taught to expect or were too young to receive the fullness of the Spirit at Confirmation. But this argument will hardly do for those Baptists who have been baptized as believers and yet are now experiencing the 'baptism' of the Spirit as an additional extra.

Furthermore, the 'Baptism of the Spirit' does not negate the Anglican experience of baptism either. There are Anglicans in the Charismatic Movement who were truly converted and have been experiencing the touch of God in all their adult lives; for them the 'Baptism of the Spirit' has been a part of their spiritual development, but by no means the whole. Some Anglican Charismatics believe that it is simply a case of realising what is ours through baptism, a release of the Holy Spirit that was given us then, but which has not fully taken possession of us because we have not surrendered to the Lordship of Christ in every area of our life; hence the emphasis in the Movement on submission to the Lordship of Christ. This is certainly true to the experience of some people, but is it the whole explanation? For others it has come unexpectedly as an answer to prayer about knowing how to pray, or knowing how to deal with a situation, or simply praying about the way forward, or as an anointing for ministry or mission.

Some Anglo-Catholics think that the Charismatic experience is acceptable because the Pope prayed for a second Pentecost for the Church, and they see it as an answer to that prayer. In the Roman Catholic Church, however, which has been more deeply affected by the Charismatic Movement than any other denomination, the difficulty that has been felt is that of understanding an experience of the Spirit which has not come directly through one of the Sacraments. Francis A. Sullivan SJ, in his book *Charisms and the Charismatic Renewal*, comes to the conclusion from biblical and theological study that people are receiving a fresh outpouring of the Spirit in answer to prayer, but that this does not in any way mean that they have not received the Spirit at initiation, nor indeed that they could not receive further outpourings of the Spirit in the future. He draws an analogy with ordination—although the ordinand is a fully baptised, confirmed, committed Christian, the Church still prays for a further anointing of the Spirit to confer the grace of ordination. He says (p. 75) 'I am convinced that there will never be a time during our pilgrimage on earth when the Lord could not give us a powerful new gift of the Spirit that would really move us into some new act or new state of grace'.

The writer of Acts would entirely agree with him. Immediately after Pentecost the newly born Church faces its first crisis (Acts 4), when the disciples are forbidden to speak or teach in the name of Jesus. They give themselves to prayer, and, even though they have just received the Spirit, the prayer is answered by a second filling of the Spirit, after which they 'speak the word with boldness' (Acts 4. 31).

The problems seem to arise among those on both sides who think that encountering God in one particular way is the whole story, and who restrict the possibility of God's action to what they have themselves experienced. The Charismatic form of this temptation is to think that speaking in tongues is the hallmark of the spiritual person, and that until you do this you have not quite 'made it'. St Paul makes it quite clear to the Corinthian Church that although he speaks in tongues 'more than you all' the hallmark of the spiritual person is love. On the other hand the critique of the Movement which interprets tongue-speaking as simply auto-suggestion, produced by the expectations of the Movement, is not borne out by the evidence of those outside the Movement, who have had no teaching or expectation of the gift of tongues, but have nonetheless received it in answer to petition about how to pray.

If one uses the traditional yardstick to assess the presence and working of the Holy Spirit (that it is purgative, illuminative and unitive), then the contemporary evidence of the wider Church indicates that people are receiving the Holy Spirit experientially or otherwise, with speaking in tongues and without it, but that one does not necessarily invalidate the other. Indeed the Charismatic experience seems to bear the best fruit in those who have been well grounded in another tradition. Bishop Pat Harris commented that he thought the clergy who had been brought up purely within the Charismatic ethos were not as balanced and wise as the first Anglican Charismatic leaders like Prebendary John Collins or Canon Michael Harper, who had a solid Evangelical basis.

'They should praise God and move on' says Martin Israel. 'I believe in the experience all right, but not always with their understanding of it. I believe it is a psychic opening of a person who has been closed, either intellectually or psychically; certainly it opens the psychic centres (of which the Church is very ignorant) for good or ill, and the power of the Spirit enters them. If the power is of God, and that is the important thing, it is real. But some people think that tongues are the apogee of prayer—they aren't, but they are a marvellous way of leading into the prayer of quiet and into contemplation. Their experience gives assurance, which is good, but it also makes them judgemental. If only they would get on and do their thing and love others. You can be right, but out of balance; the Charismatic Movement needs to integrate into the rest of the Church and be informed by its theology, and at some time inform the Church of its own theology. As we have learned, so we give'.

There are healthy signs that this is happening more and more—the convergence between the Charismatic Movement and the Meditation Movement is helping some Charismatics to see their spirituality in a wider context. 'It is exciting to discover and be enlarged' said a Charismatic who is doing this. In a different way the convergence with the Radicals is also proving fruitful. But Charismatics are still meeting rebuff in some quarters, and feel that they are not yet being taken seriously. From the other side of the fence there are accusations of being 'lightweight' and of 'arrogance and super-spirituality'. It needs what a religious called 'an *ascesis* of listening to one another and acts of love for one another' on both sides if this integration is to continue to make progress. Contributions to theology by Anglican Charismatics are still comparatively few, in contrast to the Roman Catholic Church, where the Movement has had more impact among intellectuals. The helpful magazine produced by Tom Smail, *Theology of Renewal*, is unfortunately no longer being published.

A healthy sign is an increased willingness to face the shadow side of life; to encounter positively the darker side of our nature and to face the mystery of suffering and death. The August/September 1985 edition of *Renewal* magazine, an inter-denominational magazine of the Charismatic Movement, carried five articles about the facing of innocent suffering, and a reminder

77

in its editorial that we must not construct a spirituality that excludes a Cross. This is a change of note from the earlier more triumphalist days of the Movement. Many people in the Church have been slogging on without much hope or expectation; it is all Cross without Resurrection, let alone Pentecost. Charismatic renewal restores this balance, and brings greater joy and freedom; but it can sometimes slip into the other extreme, an unreal escapism.

A clergyman described his renewal as a Transfiguration experience. 'We do not understand the Transfiguration', says Martin Israel. 'It's not a matter of rising above the difficulties'. What was being discussed on the top of the mountain—something which in the three Synoptic accounts is only mentioned in Luke (Luke 9. 31)—was what Jesus was about to accomplish through his death in Jerusalem. It looks forward to the climax of the struggle through which God's kingdom will be established and a new community of God's people will be founded. Suffering, death, new life, new order and new community are all part of the pattern as God renews his covenant with his people. Renewal requires a raising of the level of faith so that the person or community can face the difficulties and overcome them, but the emphasis in all the renewal movements is on achieving this not with our own strength, but as we open ourselves to God's grace and power.

Another clergyman came to see Canon Donald Allchin. He was worried because so many of his parishioners were in tears. 'The gift of tears is better documented than the gift of tongues', said Donald Allchin reassuringly. And indeed it used to be thought of as the very hallmark of devotion, a sign that God was at work. Even more reassuring, during my visits to parishes, was to see the gift of laughter. When people stop taking themselves too seriously and see the funny side of themselves, that is a breakthrough. Last, but by

78

no means least, spiritual experience today often carries with it an anointing for ministry and mission, conferring not just a new walk with God, but also a new enabling power to help fulfil a missionary role within the body of Christ and within the environment. Such experience may deepen prayer life, but it also turns people outwards towards their neighbours and towards society. They are full of new energy which needs to be channelled in the right direction if it is to bear fruit. This can be a problem for lay people, who sometimes may not be in a situation where they will get the support and training they need, and where they can exercise a fulfilling ministry.

A bishop described what happens in a landmark-experience of spiritual renewal as being like the welling-up of a gusher when you strike it. 'It needs to be capped, but the gusher is necessary because it shows us that the oil is there ... but it terrifies me!'

Another bishop describes the Charismatic experience as being like the *ruach*, the powerful blowing of the wind of the Spirit, in contrast to the *pneuma*, the quiet gentle breathing of the Spirit.

An appropriate structure is needed to contain and channel the new energy, so that it can fuel the creative working of the Christian community. All attempts to engineer renewal structurally without this new resurgence of spiritual energy will fail, because the dynamic will be lacking; but structure is needed to tap the source of energy without either quenching it, or causing an explosion. All forms of Church are an attempt to provide this structure, to surround the holy with safeguards, checks and balances while preserving the sacred springs from which the Christian community draws its life.

Religious tradition keeps at bay those nights of glory that might otherwise engulf all of life. Whatever else it is, religious experience is dangerous. Its dangers are reduced and routinized by means of institutionalization. Religious ritual, for example, assigns the encounters with sacred reality to certain times and places, and puts them under the control of typically prudent functionaries. By the same token, religious ritual liberates the rest of life from the burden of having to undergo these encounters. The individual, thanks to religious ritual, can now go about his ordinary business—making love, making war, making a living, and so on—without being constantly interrupted by messengers from another world.

(*The Heretical Imperative: Contemporary Possibilities of Religious Affirmation*: Peter Berger, p. 50)

But, as Carter Lindberg says in his Report for the Lutheran World Federation, *Charismatic Renewal and the Lutheran Tradition*:

The problem, of course, is that the preservers and bearers of the religious experience, ensconced in tradition, too frequently succeed all too well in domesticating the experience!

Religion can become a way of keeping God at bay. The ritual becomes routine, the Spirit is quenched, the Spring reduces to a trickle, or dries up. The cutting edge of the message is lost and ceases to have the necessary impact; decline sets in. The way back that Spiritual Renewal tries to find is through the rediscovery of the primary religious experience. Peter Berger says:

To say then, that the weakening of tradition must lead to a new attention to experience is not just a theoretical proposition. Rather, it serves to explain what has actually taken place. (ibid. p. 33).

Carter Lindberg comments:

The very dynamism of the religious experience, which all renewal movements are impelled to share, is a disrupting dynamic. The charismatic, of whatever period, has in some degree been transported outside or beyond the bound-

aries of the normal institutions of life, including the
Church. The result is a different perception, which, in
turn, is disturbing to those who have not experienced it. A
fundamental reason for this tension between renewal
movements and the established churches is the awareness
that religious experience threatens the social order and
the very business of living. This was vividly illustrated by
Thomas Ollintzer and Melchior Hoffman in the Reformation period; and, while the socio-political status quo has
not been so violently challenged by Pietism and the
present renewal, there is still the awareness that religious
experience may radically relativize ordinary life!

The Charismatic contribution of raw and fresh primary
religious experience is a needed reminder both of the
community's origins and of the fact that the Christian
faith is not solely an intellectual enterprise ... The
charismatic renewal has the potential to recall us to
Luther's own insights, into the depth, mystery and
numinous character of the 'holy'.

Wherever it occurs, spiritual experience needs to be
expressed, and not just in words. It looks for expression first of all within the Christian community, where
it would expect to find affirmation and embodiment.
But the checks and balances that are designed to guard
the holy can also act as barriers which prevent any
further development. Whether the new spiritual energy
is able to revive the existing community or whether a
new community is needed to embody it depends on the
guardians of the tradition, and whether they are willing
to open the existing channels to the new life.

The Cursillo method is highly structured, and works
through the existing structures to motivate lay people
into mission through teaching, training and an experience of spiritual renewal. Cursillo cannot take place in
a diocese without the permission of the bishop, nor in a
parish without the approval of the clergy. The bishop
and the clergy come first to Cursillo, so that they can
experience at first hand what it is about, and the clergy

then send lay leaders from their parish to a Cursillo weekend. This ensures that those who are unsuitable or unready are not sent, and it also ensures that when the lay people get back into the parish all fired up they are not frustrated by a lack of understanding or opportunity to put into practice what they have learned, but rather that they have the support of the parish and the diocese. They are also given the support of a cell group, called an Ultreya, within which they can share their ongoing spiritual work, and receive the encouragement that will help them to persevere. They are expected to receive spiritual direction, and to pursue a regular pattern of prayer, study and action. In theory the cursillistas will find both spiritual renewal and the structure within which to work. In practice this can break down, if they move subsequently into a parish where what they have been taught is not understood. A cursillista who had done this told me, 'My vicar doesn't accept anything that is not within his system'. But she was able to join in with an Ultreya in a neighbouring parish.

In contrast to Cursillo, the Charismatic Movement and the Meditation Movement are spontaneous movements, which have to find their way in and out of the structures as best they may. The Meditation Movement, based as it is on a more traditional kind of spirituality, sits more easily within a traditional setting, particularly an Anglo-Catholic one; but those who are entering this area seem to be having difficulty in finding both the support and teaching they need, and the expression that they are looking for, within the confines of parish life. The growth of the Retreat Movement provides an infrastructure that they can come out to, but spiritual direction is still hard to find. One person told me, 'I have to go 200 miles to get spiritual direction, which means I don't get it very often. I am grateful for the help my spiritual director gives me, but every time I go

to him I think "Why do I have to go all this way?" ' It
may be equally a case of going miles to find the nearest
contemplative prayer group. And if they are motivated
into lay ministry, as frequently happens, it will equally
be a matter of hit or miss as to whether the parish
and/or the diocese is geared up to providing the
necessary training and opportunities. Some dioceses
are doing a great deal, others very little. And there is
similar variation in the parishes. The same problems
face those who have encountered the 'lay awakening'
through the experience of more traditional parish life.

The Charismatic Movement also lacks structure, and
has even more difficulty 'getting in' to the existing
structure, because it is an even more radical departure
from the norm. Unless the vicar is sympathetic there is
little chance of a charismatic group even being tolerated within the congregation, and the only really
effective charismatic renewal has been that which is
clergy-led. But there is now much more infrastructure
and a more extensive network outside the parishes, and
new structures are emerging within charismatic parishes to facilitate growth and to enable the new
resources and energy to be harnessed. The early days of
pioneering are over, when Charismatics were driving
into uncharted territory with more enthusiasm than
experience and when many mistakes were made. The
older hands will tell you, 'We've made our mistakes and
we've learnt from them,' and there is now much more
in the way of resources and experience to draw on.
New models and principles are beginning to emerge,
though a letter from John Richards in *Anglicans for
Renewal* pointed out that there is still a hit-and-miss
attitude to Spirit-baptism which does not give enough
thought to context, co-ordination and integration with
the Christian community. (*Anglicans for Renewal*, Autumn 1985, p. 23).

Spiritual renewal taps the root of vocation and

releases a spring of spiritual energy through which the life of the individual and the community can be renewed, but how it is received and channelled is essential to the fulfilment of the process. What happens next is crucial.

DETAILS OF SOURCES QUOTED

'Blessed be God': Poem by Jan Fortune-Wood, not previously published.

The Fourth Day: (Cursillo magazine), Issue No. 8, December 1984; Issue No. 9, March 1985.

The River Within: Christopher Bryant SSJE. Darton, Longman and Todd, London, 1978.

'Impressionistic View of the Influence of the Charismatic Renewal in the life of the Church of England': article by John Gunstone in *Strange Gifts*: ed. Martin and Mullen, Blackwell, Oxford, 1982.

Charisms and the Charismatic Renewal: Francis A. Sullivan SJ. Servant Books, Ann Arbor, Michigan, USA, 1982.

Renewal magazine: August/September 1985 edition.

The Open Church: Jürgen Moltmann, SCM Press, London, 1978.

The Julian Meetings—Tenth Anniversary Magazine: March 1984.

The Renewal of the Church: W.A. Visser t'Hooft. Dale Lectures 1958.

The Heretical Imperative, Contemporary Possibilities of Religious Affirmation: Peter Berger. Doubleday, New York, 1979.

Charismatic Renewal and the Lutheran Tradition: Carter Lindberg. Lutheran World Federation.

Anglicans for Renewal: article by John Richards in Autumn 1985 edition.

Chapter 5

THE COMMUNITY

In Search of a Roundtable

Concerning the why and how and what and who
of ministry,
One image keeps surfacing:

A table that is round.

It will take some sawing
to be roundtabled,
some redefining
and redesigning.
Some redoing and rebirthing
of narrowlong Churching
can painful be
for people and tables.
It would mean no daising
and throning,
for but one king is there,
and he was a footwasher,
at table no less.

And what of narrowlong ministers
when they confront
a roundtable people,
after years of working up the table
to finally sit at its head,

only to discover
that the table has been turned round?

They must be loved into roundness,
for God has called a People,
not 'them and us'.
'Them and us'
are unable
to gather round,
for at a roundtable,
there are no sides
and ALL are invited
to wholeness and to food.

At one time

our narrowlong Churches
were built to resemble the cross
but it does no good
for buildings to do so,
if lives do not.

Roundtabling means
no preferred seating,
no first and last,
not better, and no corners
for the 'least of these'.
Roundtabling means
being with,
a part of,
together, and one.
It means room for the Spirit
and gifts
and disturbing profound peace for all.

We can no longer prepare for the past.

We will and must and are called
to be Church,
and if He calls for other than roundtable
we are bound to follow.

Leaving the sawdust
and chips, designs and redesigns
behind,

in search of and in the presence of
the Kingdom
that is His and not ours.

Amen.

If you visit the little round Church of Santa
Constanza in Rome, what is most striking is not that it is
one of the most important examples of early Christian
architecture in Rome, nor its very real charm, nor even
the beauty of the fourth-century mosaics depicting a
grapevine motif on the vault of the circular ambulatory
surrounding the domed central space of the altar,
which stands right in the centre of the Church. What
hits you is how extraordinarily contemporary it feels. It
expresses in architectural form the shape of the
congregational structure towards which today's renewal is taking us. Fifteen hundred years seem to melt
away—this is where it is now, or where the Church is
going. The priest and the altar stand right in the centre,
at the heart of the congregation, who are grouped
around in immediate and close contact with them.
Because of the size and the shape of the building, no
one is distanced from the centre. It was built originally
as a tomb for the daughter of the Emperor Constantine, but it gives us a glimpse into the pre-Constantine
period, when Christians must have literally gathered
round in groups in their houses or in small gatherings
in the Catacombs, before the huge basilicas were built
or converted to accommodate the enormous numbers
of people who joined the Church after the Emperor
Constantine declared Christianity the state religion. We
seem to be turning back into a pre-Constantine kind of
Church, a Church of the little apostolic communities,
with profound and far-reaching consequences for our
community life and structure. In this period of
transition there is a search for community, for new

89

ways of belonging, and for an appropriate structure within which this can happen. Meanwhile there is a great deal of mismatch, and consequent frustration.

'It's as much as I can do to stay in the Church of England'. The laywoman who had been introduced to me after the Communion service was a lifelong Christian, who was trying to relate her faith to her life, but finding the Church in which she had been brought up totally stifling and frustrating.

At another Church of England church I found the opposite reaction. 'What do you think of our lovely church?' asked a layman eagerly. This church had enabled him not only to find faith, but to express it. It had supported him through a difficult time of unemployment, it had given him personal fulfilment, but it had also enabled him to give himself in worship and ministry to God and to others.

What is it that makes the Church of England so intolerable or fulfilling? What makes one laywoman talk of the sensitive and understanding leadership in the parish, and another talk of the clergy block which is preventing healthy development? Is it personalities, or simply the luck of the draw that makes one clergyman talk glowingly of how talented and gifted his congregations are, and another dismiss the laity as 'no good for mission'? Some clergy are looking for lay participation and lay leadership, but not finding it; setting the parish alight is like trying to light a soggy and reluctant bonfire—no amount of matches and paper will get it going. Others are worried by the threat of a takeover from a highly active and articulate laity. Like parents of adolescents, they are frightened to let them off the leash for fear of what they might get up to—and sometimes with good reason! In some parishes renewal is working away slowly, in others it is spreading rapidly, outstripping the resources of the parishes to cope with it. In the theological colleges I visited I found that the ordinands who were committed to some form of renewal were sceptical about the parishes they were being trained for, and about their willingness to change; but elsewhere I found individuals and groups longing and praying for parish renewal. Many lay people I talked to felt imprisoned by the Christian community structures we now have, but found it difficult to see a way forward. Many clergy too are unhappy and frustrated, but are cautious about initiating any kind of change. If a mechanism like a car goes wrong, one looks at the dials and the engine to find out what is the matter; but how does one assess community structure to know what is amiss, and what is needed to put things right? In the present state of dissatisfaction with forms of Church life, there is a variety of approaches.

Those who are involved in spiritual renewal have diagnosed the fault as a spiritual one, i.e. that the petrol tank is dry, or at a dangerously low ebb, and they concentrate on filling the tank, and keeping it filled. It may be that all that is needed to get the engine coughing back into life is an injection of spiritual petrol. 'Parishes suddenly switch on', said a diocesan missioner. If you look behind the scenes in a parish that has experienced an awakening you often find that a person or a group has started to pray with new energy, life and hope. I was told by a religious about a parish that had been renewed 'by the power of prayer alone'. An Evangelical Charismatic vicar told me, 'They (the other clergy) think that we only represent swinging from the chandeliers, and banging of tambourines, but we had to do away with our chandeliers when we enlarged the building to get more people in ... They do not actually know what makes us tick at all. Fortunately our bishops do parish visitations and visit for the whole weekend. Our bishop came, and at the end of the weekend he said, 'I can see what your secret is, a lot of

91

prayer, and a lot of jolly hard work'. But the vicar added, 'I was trained in office management, Air Force style. I was in a backroom job of organising major European exercises where we used the Ops Block—organising invasion and escape exercises and going to aircrew stations to plan it all. In all honesty, I think if I didn't have all that knowledge of what makes an office and a unit of organisation work, renewal would not have happened with us in the way it did.'

As parishes engaged in spiritual renewal have found, there are structural problems that have to be solved too. Pumping on the accelerator can simply flood an engine that is stuck for structural reasons; blockages have to be dealt with, structural designs ought to be appropriate to the needs of the community, and they require careful management.

On the other hand, some tend to take the spiritual dimension for granted, to look first and foremost for structural problems, to send for the behavioural scientists, group dynamics experts, management consultants, and so on. They can shed helpful light on the nature of some of the problems, though they tend to be better at diagnosis than cure. In one of the Peanuts cartoons Charlie Brown complains to Lucy that in playing the part of psychiatrist, she had not given him an answer to his problem. 'I don't give answers' replies Lucy, 'I just tell you what the problem is'. It is precisely because group dynamics, sociology and related disciplines have not proved to be a means of salvation, that some people have turned to spiritual renewal. But petrol for the tank *and* a healthy engine will have to be found if the car is to move forward.

At this point the car analogy breaks down, because we are not talking about a mechanical object, but a delicate pattern of relationship. The Holy Spirit is not merely a source of power which requires the pressing of the right buttons to tap and manipulate, but a

Person, God seeking relationship with us. A Charismatic clergyman let slip the phrase 'God is working for us' in talking to me. I think he meant that the *Gospel* was working, but the way he expressed it revealed the temptation that is so easy to fall into—of seeing God, as well as other people, as a means of achieving an end, as tools to be used for encompassing a (maybe) worthy aim. Management science distinguishes different styles of management as being either task-oriented or people-oriented. But for the Church people *are* the task. Making relationships with God, with each other and with the wider community are the primary pieces of work that have to be done. Becoming more efficient at organisation may help to oil the machinery in one area of the community's life, but does not in itself give an appropriate structure for relationships to develop in a way that characterises the Body of Christ. How can we build an authentic Christian community that expresses the ideals, the aspirations, the theology, the spirituality of today? What is the distinctive nature of a contemporary Christian community which is of today, but which prefigures the Kingdom?

Phil Bradshaw, Community Convenor, asks in the *Community of Celebration Newsletter* (September 1985):

> What are the characteristics of a 'Kingdom' environment? In very broad terms we might identify two aspects. First, it is a place where individual giftedness—our personal uniqueness—is offered to God and to each other. This implies the recognition that human gifts are vehicles to reveal the glory of God (which will not be revealed if we withhold them), and that they are only vehicles; they do not exist for their own sake. Second, the body of Christ must have a goal outside itself, which is to be the visible expression of the gospel to the world.
>
> Taken together, these two aspects imply a way of life that is both distinctive *and* rooted in society, i.e. not a religious

ghetto. The earth is the Lord's and humankind are its stewards; 'Occupy till I come' (Luke 19. 13) is the command. In Jesus' parable of the husbandmen, however, God leaves the world in the charge of servants who lost sight of the fact that they are his servants. Many Christians today have also lost sight of the fact that they are his servants. Many Christians today have also lost sight of the concept of serving the world. They may even be antagonistic to the very idea. Others particularise it by serving some cause or other. But the Church is not called to a cause. Its glory is in the different dimension that it brings to the ordinary things of everyday life, both great and small.

The idea of living eternal life now is sometimes confused with a head-in-the-clouds kind of piety. Nevertheless, our perspective does make a great deal of practical difference to the way we live. If we consider the span of natural life as the sum total of our lives, we will find ourselves confronted constantly with our despair, which in practical terms means that goals and achievements will be of primary importance. From the perspective of eternity, however, the manner and quality of our living is more important than the tasks we have completed. This is because the body of Christ, in the midst of which we live our lives together with all the saints, is a living organism. Its essence is not to fulfil tasks, but to be 'to the praise of his glory' (Ephesians 1. 12).

I found that people are looking for a community where they can encounter God and each other, but that our structures are often a hindrance rather than a help in this, and are consequently felt to be oppressive. Spiritual renewal, however, not only fills the tank with petrol; it also changes people. And as people change, their relationships begin to change; and as relationships change, there is a shift in community structures. The attempt to impose structural reform without inner change leads to mismatch—it forces people to wear something that does not fit. Liturgical renewal has run into this difficulty when it has been imposed on a community that has not moved into the contemporary understanding of spirituality and community which the new liturgy is endeavouring to express. Spiritual renewal without structural reform leads to equal discomfort. People start to grow and change, and to burst through the old structures, which are no longer appropriate. 'Don't cut the person to fit the coat', says Anthony de Mello (*The Song of the Bird*). The present frustration in all the Churches relates to both kinds of mismatch. After a long period of immobility, we are trying to move different kinds of people along together in the same community. What is too fast for some is too slow for others, and yet this is a time when the rate of change is outstripping the most energetic efforts that are being made to cope with it.

The most fundamental change taking place lies in the very fabric of the Church community, the web of relationship that binds it together. A bishop has outlined three different stages through which he perceived parishes to be moving:

Stage 1—the vicar is the Church and he does it all.

Stage 2—the lay people are here to help the vicar run the parish.

Stage 3—the vicar is here to help the lay people to be the Church.

In a Stage 1 Church, the structure is hierarchical, and within its pyramidal constraints the activity is limited by what the vicar can do or run himself. Theologically it is based on an emphasis on the Fatherhood of God, and the dynamic flow, both in this particular Trinitarian model, and in this particular parish model, is mainly from the apex of the pyramid downwards. The theology and the structure are closely linked, as can be seen from these two diagrams:

95

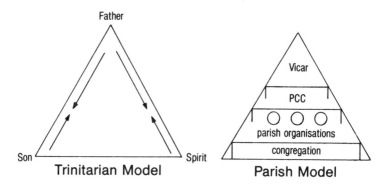

Trinitarian Model   **Parish Model**

'It is difficult to imagine a parish without lay participation', said a diocesan missioner. But perceptions of what this participation might be are varied. There is a sense in which to go to a service and join in the prayers and hymns is participation; but it can be a passive role, with little room for expression or involvement, while the activity is carried by one person or by a handful of people, who (unless they are particularly skilful) may reduce the rest to apathetic spectators.

The role of the vicar in such a parish was described to me by a clergyman as being 'The Lone Ranger without even Tonto!' This suits those lay people who wish to be passive, receiving or parented, or who wish to distance themselves from involvement. But young people tend to leave as soon as they reach adolescence, because at that stage they are resisting being parented. It also serves the needs of the dwindling number of people who (as David Prior says in his book *The Church in the Home*), treat the Church as a kind of supermarket to which they can come for baptisms, marriages and funerals. But such a Church is an historic relic of a bygone age, and parishes of this kind are finding it increasingly hard to survive, though they still exist. A mission sister told me that she was sent to one in which she felt she was going back fifty years in time. There was little or no lay participation or involvement.

Lay people who come to life in such a parish may have either to leave, or to look to extra-parochial structures to fulfil their needs, or to give their real gifts to the Body of Christ, because the parish is still geared to running the Sunday Service, the Sunday School, perhaps a youth club, and the occasional social, distinguishable only as a Christian gathering by the dutiful presence of the vicar. It gives little scope to those who wish for more opportunity to grow in adult discipleship and prayer life, or to exercise lay ministry, or to engage in mission. Efforts by the laity to inject new life will be opposed or contained by the vicar, who tends to be uneasy about anything not run or initiated by himself. Being continually preached at, 'six foot above contradiction' in the pulpit (as one laywoman put it), with little or no opportunity for dialogue or discussion, only increases the frustration that the livelier souls in such a congregation may feel. So in such a parish the impact of spiritual renewal on the laity may either be inhibited by the structure and prevent further growth or development taking place, or will lead to displacement, as the lay person looks outside the parish to where the 'real life' is for the means to growth. The extra-parochial communities that I visited, both in the Retreat and Meditation Movements and in the Charismatic Movement, were catering for many lay people who found themselves in this position. The other alternative is to leave altogether and join another Anglican Church, or the Church House Movement. A diocesan missioner quoted a typical case of a charismatic group leaving a Stage 1 Church, pronouncing it to be 'dull and void'.

The other side to this coin is that clergy who inherit a parish like this but who want greater lay involvement

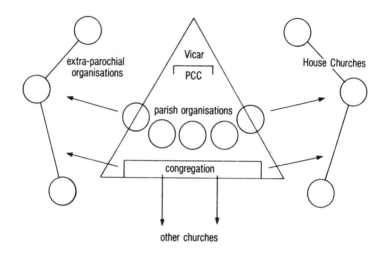

face an uphill task, since many of those who are left in
the congregation have been conditioned by years of
passivity or downright apathy, or are happy with the
situation because they want minimal commitment and
involvement, and do not wish to change. The vicar of a
parish engaged in Charismatic Renewal described his
predecessor as having dragged the parish kicking and
screaming into the twentieth century; apparently these
strong-arm tactics had paved the way for still further
changes, but only against further bitter opposition.
However, both clergy and laity in a Stage 1 parish
reflect what they have been given, and there is a lot of
history lying behind this model.

A willingness to respond to change on the part of
clergy and laity may bring about a mutation in the
community structure, so that it will now begin to fit the
bishop's description of a Stage 2 Church—when the lay

people are there to help the vicar run the Church. In the parishes I have studied that have moved from Stage 1 to Stage 2 through spiritual renewal this has happened because of two factors.

The first is that the presence of spiritual renewal within a parish seems to attract people from outside who require much time-consuming ministry. The vicar soon finds that he cannot cope single-handed with the demands being made. He then is faced with a choice—either to withdraw from this ministry which is consuming more and more of his energies to the exclusion of other necessary tasks, and turn his back on the need; or to train lay people within the parish to share the workload with him. Pastoral concern for those seeking help gives him a strong incentive to start enabling and training others to share his ministry, so that the needs can be met. The crucial factor here is whether he has the confidence to share his ministry with others and to accept the risk that they are going to make mistakes for which he will then have to take full responsibility. Although he may wish in theory to bring the lay people on, he may in practice not be skilled as a trainer, and the effectiveness of the community's ministry may be inhibited by his lack of confidence in sharing his ministry, or in deputising, or by a lack of effective training, or commitment to it. The Director of a Diocesan Shared Ministry Project said to me that the insecurity and unsureness of clergy makes them close up against the laity, because they lack the confidence to share ministry. 'It's all a question of confidence'. He saw the Shared Ministry Project's job as being:

(1) Giving lay people the confidence to do it.

(2) Helping the parish to see that it is O.K.

(3) Enabling the clergy to let go.

He found that the bishop's commissioning gave confidence, but stressed that training was essential. The vicar of a parish which is developing a lay training centre said to his fellow-clergy, 'It's not working yourself out of a job, it's working harder than ever! Blow away the smoke and fan the flames. Have the courage to say, "This is daft", if you think something is. Let out the leash and bring it in again. Train, train, train!'

Clergy are frequently discouraged from this course of action because they think that leadership material is not there in the parish. The Rev. Clarry Hendrickse stresses in his helpful Grove booklet, *One Inner Urban Church and Lay Ministry* (Grove Pastoral Series No. 13) that it is essential not to give up or be discouraged because people are not where we want them to be. 'The key to training the laity is the minister. He must want the laity to be trained, and believe that they can be trained'. He found that it was possible to bring on lay people into participation, leadership and ministry in a deprived area, although he was told, 'There is no leadership material down there'. But it took much time, priority of effort, patience, and long-term commitment, plus a willingness to use local resources for training.

Another factor is at work where spiritual renewal is taking place that will influence the community structure. Both inside and outside the Church the small group movement has been emerging, the setting up of units within which people can relate, share and engage in a task. The small group movement attempts to overcome the isolation that people feel in our society as part of the anonymous herd. Groups coming together for a religious purpose, such as prayer, Bible study, or meditation, are a feature of those parts of the Church where there is a 'coming-to-life' of the laity. But they are an effect, rather than a cause. Groups like these tend to spring up in the wake of spiritual renewal, and efforts to generate them because they are the thing nowadays meet with disappointment, if the parish is not ready for them. The experience of an awakening, however, opens people up and allows them to meet in a group that will give them space to share and grow in understanding with those on the same path—it is an indication of the new life pushing up to the surface and looking for nourishment and expression. In this close fellowship there can often be greater scope for participation and expression by individuals than is ever possible in a larger gathering.

But as individuals involved in spiritual renewal move into the group stage, they can again meet with blocks within parish life. Some clergy are anxious about allowing small groups like this to hive off from the main body without their direct control and participation; but if they come, they will turn the group into something quite different. Their presence in the group will change it into a teacher/pupil situation, with the pupils hanging back and letting the teacher make all the running, whereas one of the things that the participants need is a peer-group in which they can all share. The teaching group is also needed, but this is a different exercise. The early Methodists distinguished in their group structure between *the band*, the small peer group without a formal leader, which acted as a kind of group confessional, *the class*, which was a teaching group with a trained leader, and *the society*, which was the equivalent of the congregation, with the minister in charge. As the number of groups grows in a parish, it will in any case become impossible for the vicar to attend them all; he will be forced either to close them down, or to let go and enable lay people to take the leadership role. Lay people too must be willing to let go, and to accept leadership and ministry from each other, rather than look to the vicar for everything.

Some parishes who are involved in structural as well

as spiritual renewal have adopted the Church Growth
model of *cell, congregation, celebration*. In this type of
structure the parish is made up of small cell groups of
eight to a dozen people, in which the participants meet
under the supervision of a lay pastor. These are linked
and meet regularly in medium-sized groups for more
directive teaching and worship, with the help of clergy.
These medium-sized groups are linked to the whole
congregation, which then becomes the celebration
level. This in theory gives opportunities for more
intimate fellowship, personal relationship with a lay
pastor, teaching from a trained leader, and identifica-
tion with the larger body, preventing the groups
becoming inward-looking and isolationist.

I visited a number of multi-celled parishes of this
type in very different community settings, varying in
size from eight to over a hundred groups. I found that
to differing degrees they were meeting the needs of
people who were experiencing spiritual renewal,
though with difficulty. There is a high failure rate
among the groups which, according to one vicar,
'frequently collapse with loud rattling noises'. The
difficulties seem to arise because the function and
needs of the groups have not been understood or
identified clearly enough, and their leadership is either
too directive, unskilled, or imposed from above, and
not the natural leadership that the group will follow.
'Calling people pastors and putting them in charge of a
group doesn't necessarily mean that people will go to
them for help and advice', said a member of a Pastoral
Leadership Group. Even in the Charismatic parishes,
where one would expect a special emphasis to be given
to gifts, there was not enough attention directed to
using the special giftedness of the members of the
groups. In working-class parishes more encouragement
and help was needed to get cell groups off the ground,
because the leaders tended to lack confidence and to

give up when problems arose, rather than working through them. In one parish I visited, a cultural mix was causing difficulties; the less confident working-class people were quite unconsciously being elbowed out by the more articulate middle-class members, and felt that their voice was not being heard. But in general I found that the claim that groups do not flourish in a working-class parish was false. They can and do work, if the clergy are committed to helping them to persevere and are willing to stand alongside the mistakes that are made.

In spite of frequent failure, stereotyping, and neglect of the less confident and articulate lay people by some of the groups, I found that this structure was giving enough scope for at least some people to grow, to develop and in some cases to begin to flower in creativity and leadership. The energy and new life given by spiritual renewal can be given some shape and direction by this method. If there were greater clarity of definition and more training in the skills needed for leadership, it would function still better and in a less ad hoc fashion.

Leadership that is imposed from outside the group, rather than arising from within it, will—unless it is very sensitive—stifle the group agenda, rather than help the members to work through it and take them forward. The rationale of the grass-roots, basic Christian communities of the Third World, which are designed to help ordinary people to interpret their own experiences prayerfully and in the light of the Gospel, is being studied by some Christian leaders here; but it has not been generally accepted, even among those who are most committed to renewal. We still want to start where *we* want to be, rather than where people are, and then we tend to be disappointed when they do not respond. The clergy are trained to work through directive teaching, rather than through an enabling, training

103

role; so the balance between the need for Christian fellowship, sharing teaching training, and employment in an appropriate task is being achieved to a very varying degree. In one parish I visited, the vicar had attempted to bring the parish into renewal by bringing individuals into an experience of spiritual renewal, and also by working with the whole community together, without going through the group stage where individual needs could be met. He had lost a group of young people to the House Church Movement, most probably for this reason.

The small group can be the place in which individual needs are met, in which people can grow spiritually, and (if enabled) move out into ministry and mission, but both the individual and the group need to work their way through to this. Clergy who are unwilling to let small groups meet in the parish, or who impose the wrong agenda or leadership on such groups, can stifle the new life and growth that could arise. Clergy themselves often feel stifled by the role that they are expected to play, and feel that the Church is imposing its agenda on them, rather than enabling them to do their job as they see it. One of them said to me, 'The biggest disappointment of my ministry has been that no one in authority over me has ever sat down and said, "What is it that you are trying to do, and how can I help?" ' Some bishops, already overworked and over-stretched, have complained of the additional agenda imposed on them by General Synod; this is seen as yet another burden, instead of a problem-solving exercise that can help the wider church community to function better. The process of stifling the agenda of the group, instead of taking them forward from where they are, is something that I found happening at every level in the Church, and seems to be a major cause of present dissatisfaction with structures and leadership.

If the Gospel, the tradition, and a servant ministry

are what the Church believes them to be, then they are keys with which to unlock our agenda, to interpret our experience, and to take it forward. But where in the Church of England is there an academic theologian of the calibre of Jürgen Moltmann, willing to stand alongside the laity in the congregation, to do theology from their perspective, to articulate and interpret their viewpoint with his expertise, to remember what it is like to be 'Volk', rather than to impose his own agenda from above? Or where in the hierarchy is a bishop who identifies with his people so that he can say with Archbishop Oscar Romero:

> I believe that the bishop has much to learn from the people. Precisely in those charisms that the Holy Spirit gives to his people the bishop finds the touchstone of his authenticity.
>
> 9 September 1979
> (*The Church is All of You: Thoughts of Archbishop Oscar Romero*, translated by James Brockman).

'The maturation of the congregation is still the unfinished work of the Reformation', says Douglas Meeks in his introduction to Moltmann's *The Open Church*. How is the present leadership in the Church to enable the laity to mature graciously into the full stature of their calling in Christ? I found a tug-of-war going on between some clergy and laity similar to that which operates between parents and their adolescent children. The laity, often awkward and difficult, pushing towards greater freedom and expression; some clergy possessive, frightened to let go, anxious about their offspring; but others encouraging them to get on with it, looking for maturity and leadership.

'We are all *laos*, and we all have a ministry', said a religious. But the Church as a whole is still a long way from recognising this, and from enabling it to happen. Some lay people are only too happy to sit back in the pew and let the vicar and a few eager-beavers get on

105

with it; but when spiritual renewal moves them into a more active Christian life, the question of training, integration and employment becomes an urgent one. A debriefing I attended of young people who had been to a diocesan conference on vocation told its own story. The youngsters were disappointed because the conference had turned out to be a thinly-veiled attempt to produce more ordination candidates. There was no recognition that there might be a genuine vocation for lay people; apparently, only the ordained were called, and then only to a narrow understanding of what ordained ministry is. 'Lay people don't seem to matter', was the reaction.

A few initiatives are being taken to address the problems. Following the Tiller Report on Shared Ministry, the contributors to *All are Called—Towards* a *Theology of the Laity*, attempt to begin to bridge the gap between what they see as the imbalance between the attention paid to the clergy, their training and their work, and the role and theology of the laity. Two diocesan missioners have got together to put on an in-service training course for clergy to help them to work through the issues that can arise through individual and community renewal. A conference of the Association of Centres of Adult Theological Education, which I attended, was addressing the subjects of contextual theology, methodology of education, and training for collaborative ministry.

Meanwhile, back in the parish, the clergy and laity who are getting to grips with being a Stage 2 Church, having recognised that one man cannot be the whole body of Christ in one place, are trying to work through what that discovery means. It can mean that the vicar's role becomes highly managerial; instead of the congregational life depending on how many people he can minister to personally, it becomes dependent on his managerial ability, on his skills in devolving authority on others, training, co-ordinating, organising a team of lay helpers to perform the parochial tasks. If he is able to do this effectively, he will be able to widen the base of the pyramid, increase the number of groups within the structure and increase both the quality and quantity of parish life, thus:

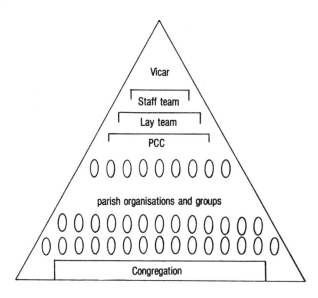

But in spite of this expansion, the parish structure is still overstretched by the demands being made on it, and the temptation for many clergy in Stage 2 parishes is to turn the newly active laity into tools to keep the parish machinery working. An eager beaver swimming into this parochial net will be snapped up and pressed into service, but not necessarily to do an appropriate task. Out of a desire to be helpful the lay person may take it on, but he or she may have little giftedness, skills or training for it, may be a square peg in a round hole, and tasks ineffectively carried out will lead to discouragement and disillusion. Some people will be run off their feet, and others will find that their true gifts are not being used, causing pockets of frustration. I found that lay women were particularly frustrated in the role being assigned to them in many charismatic churches. One complained in her parish magazine that there seemed to be little scope for women to exercise their gifts in the parish except to prophesy or to dance! That makes a change from flower arranging or pouring the coffee, but may be equally inappropriate for some. There is frequently a sense of unease, 'We are not related right, as a group or as a community' explained one layman to me.

The root of the problem is that the broad-based pyramid does not make enough allowance for the discernment of gifts. Tasks tend to be allocated from above, instead of growing out of group life. And, as Jean Vanier says (*Community and Growth*, p. 149):

> The leaders do not have a monopoly of insights and gifts; their role, on the contrary, is to help all the community's members to exercise their own gifts for the good of the whole. A community can only become a harmonious whole, with 'one heart, one soul, one spirit', if all its members are exercising their own gifts fully. If the model of their relationship to authority is worker to boss, or soldier to officer, then there is no understanding of what community means.

So as spiritual renewal begins to affect the community structure, it brings a change in the shape and the nature of the community and puts several strains on the traditional hierarchical framework. The pressure to relate in a new way brings a further mutation in the structure, away from the hierarchical model towards a more organic way of functioning. The pyramidal structure begins to disappear, and the community takes on the state of a living organism which grows and multiplies in a cellular fashion.

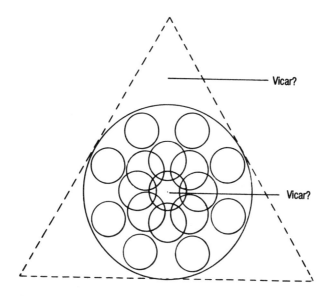

This will put severe pressure on the vicar who tries to continue to operate from an hierarchical position, in a pyramid which is changing shape beneath him. Unless he adjusts to the new situation he will find his position increasingly untenable. Sometimes clergy resist change because it feels like a threat to authority and could degenerate into a power-struggle. But what is now needed is for him to take up a central position within the circle and give a strong lead from there. If he does so his real authority will be strengthened, because he will be rightly related to the rest of the structure. He has to die to his hierarchical role, and discover a new style of leadership within the cellular groupings that now cluster around the nucleus of the developing church. It is not a case of giving way to pressure from individuals or groups, but rather of making a major adjustment in the way in which he relates to the renewed community. I visited a number of parishes which had moved from Stage 1 to Stage 2 as a result of spiritual renewal, but which had got stuck at that point because the vicar had not made this necessary adjustment to his role, and as a result frustration was growing. 'It is like water building up behind a dam wall', a laywoman said, 'One wonders what is going to happen, and whether the wall is going to give way'. I found that the build-up of pressure can lead either to the vicar looking for another parish, because the situation had become fraught, or the lay people leaving, or looking to extra-parochial situations for continuing development.

Other clergy had made the adjustment, but found themselves having to stand firm against lay people who were trying to re-introduce the hierarchical way of working. Many lay people experience the hierarchical style of leadership at work, and unconsciously transfer this to their role within the Church community, where it can cause friction. They may have had secular management training which (unlike the parish situation) makes no allowance for working with volunteers, and their style will be resented within a church setting, where there is a need to affirm one another's ministry rather than pull rank or status. In the working papers for the ACATE Conference already alluded to (p. 106), there was a reference to lay ministry assuming a hierarchical order, with those on ministry training schemes 'beginning to get out of cleaning rotas, having moved to higher things'. Some lay people I met had come back into the Anglican Church from the House Church Movement, because they had experienced there a lay leadership that was more authoritarian and overbearing than any Anglican clergyman would dream of being nowadays.

'Authority comes from what you do, not from the office', commented a vicar, 'but clergy lose a lot by keeping up a front and not sharing their difficulties with their lay people'. At an Anglican Renewal Ministries conference I attended, time was given to working in small groups. It was encouraging to see the openness in the groups, and the sensitive way in which clergy and their wives were ministering and being ministered to. But a vicar's wife said to me, 'If you come back with us into our parishes you would see the masks go back on again'. Yet, as Jean Vanier says:

> It is important for people in authority to reveal themselves as they are and to share their weaknesses. If they hide these, people may see them as an unattainable model. They have to be seen as fallible and human, but at the same time trusting and trying to grow.
> (*Community and Growth*: Jean Vanier, p. 163).

The vicar's experience and training will probably not have prepared him for the next step ahead, and naturally enough there is some casting around for models. Instead of the traditional hierarchical structure that mirrors a particular interpretation of the Fatherhood of God, an alternative structure is one that centres on the Person of Jesus, and that tries to reflect the relationship that he invites his disciples into, that of a circle of friendship. David Prior, in his book *The Church in the Home*, looks at Jesus' relationships as depicted in the Gospels, in reverse order of closeness and concentration:-

6. The crowds
5. Those who believed in him
4. The Seventy
3. The Twelve
2. Peter, James, and John, Mary, Martha, and Lazarus
1. John

Jesus was concerned about them all, but there were different levels of relationship, commitment, and closeness. There is a tendency today in some parts of the Church to exhort congregations into community by

111

telling them that they are all one Christian family, and to try to move them out of small groups, which are seen as cliques, into being all together in one large group. But the nuclear family unit is very small (on average, four), the close family will number between twelve and fifty, and there will be a much larger group that meets occasionally at weddings and funerals. We are related to them all, but we cannot relate to them all at the same level. If we want to come into deeper relationship with one another, small *is* beautiful.

Evangelical churches have tended to look to the Jesus model rather than to the Father model, and to assemble around the staff leadership a core group, who have increasingly over the past four decades taken on a share of the leadership function. All of the Evangelical and the Evangelical Charismatic churches I visited had either an eldership, or an incipient eldership group called by some other name. This was generally seen in management terms, rather than as a circle of Christian fellowship. Indeed, in those parishes where the group had not been elected by the Parochial Church Council, but had been picked by the vicar, there was uneasiness and suspicion on the part of the Parochial Church Council about their respective roles. In moving from hierarchy to a group way of working, benefits and dangers begin to emerge. Clergy have often been taught not to have particular friends within the parish, as they have to relate to the whole of the community and not just to particular groupings within it. The experience of spiritual renewal breaks down barriers and brings the nucleus of the church closer together, which can have both positive and negative results. Clergy in this position are no longer isolated and lonely, they are both giving and receiving a greater depth of Christian fellowship within the parish; but there is the danger of falling too much under the sway of one particular group and of not hearing the voice of those in the community who are not receiving such concentrated attention. Unless the new quality of relationships can be shared throughout the parish by interlocking groupings, there will be 'haves' and 'have-nots'—people who are 'in' or 'out'. This is an additional spur to accepting the multi-cellular model, which was perceived by one Evangelical Charismatic vicar like this:

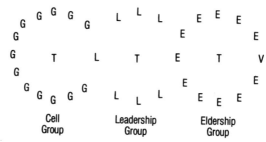

G = Group member

L = Leader

E = Elder

T = Trinity

V = Vicar

His comment about this model was, 'A few years ago we would have put Jesus in the middle of the groups, but now we put the Trinity'. This is a reflection of a shift towards Trinitarian thinking which is taking place throughout the Church. In the sixties we seemed in danger of turning into a Jesus cult; the seventies were the age of the Spirit; now in the eighties we seem to be focusing our attention again on the Trinity. It is interesting to compare the parish model above with an illustration depicting the Trinity taken from *Enfolded in Love, Daily Readings with Julian of Norwich* (Darton, Longman and Todd).

This sense of God the Trinity, in charge at the centre, the dynamic mover of the cellular groups that make up

113

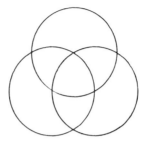

the developing organism, was very strong in the parishes that I visited where spiritual renewal had made the greatest impact. The sense of God as the absent master who has gone away, leaving the stewards in charge to cope with the situation as best they can from the blueprint he has left behind him, has been replaced by this sense that the sovereign God is here, in charge, and leading the Church into uncharted waters. He is 'the director of all that happens within the local church and within the community, and it is he who has everything under control (even if at times it does not seem like it) ... This assurance will enable (the minister) to sleep most nights!' (*One Inner Urban Church and Lay Ministry*: The Rev. Clarry Hendrickse). Clarry Hendrickse goes on to describe the second point of reference in the renewed community:

> ... the belief that baptism into Christ is the root from which all ministry grows. All Christians, by virtue of baptism, have a calling from God which has to be worked out within the fellowship of the church. The ordained minister has a particular calling of leadership which is recognised and validated by the whole church. His job is not then primarily to run around conducting ministry on behalf of the church, but so to teach and train, that he enables other church members to discover their gifts and use them for the good of all. Lay training cannot

114

therefore be regarded as an optional extra to come at the end of a whole host of seemingly more important ministries. It is *the* ministry from which all other ministries flow ... the church is corporate and can only be effective when it is enabled to express itself truly ... It is not just that every person has a unique ministry to offer within the local church, but that the total of all those ministries add up to more than the sum of their individual parts ... All gifts need to be recognised, valued and affirmed, and the less obvious gifts need to be cherished as an indispensable part of the whole ministry without which that ministry becomes incomplete and less effective.

(*One Inner Urban Church and Lay Ministry*: The Rev. Clarry Hendrickse).

This is the rationale of the Stage 3 church, in which the vicar is there to help the lay people to be the church. It requires a strong leadership which keeps the task and the nature of the church, a vision of what the church is *for*, continually before its members, but which is there as a servant ministry to help them to do it. The vicar is there to enable, not to inhibit. There is still a temptation to fall back into the Stage 2 church, and to use the people who have moved from being passive pew-warmers into being active Christians as parish fodder, to be pressed into service to keep the show on the road. They are not there to be pressed into a parish treadmill, however, but to be released into what God is bringing into being in them and among them. This means that the community must attempt to discern what God is doing, and enable that to come into fulfilment. Archbishop Oscar Romero, on 17th December 1978, said:

I know that God's spirit, who made Christ's body in Mary's womb, and keeps making the Church in history ... here in the archdiocese, is a spirit that is hovering in the words of Genesis—over a new creation.

I sense that there is something new in the archdiocese.

I am a man, frail and limited, and I do not know what is happening, but I do know that God knows.

My role as pastor is what St Paul tells me today, 'Do not quench the Spirit'.

If I say in an authoritarian way to a priest: 'Don't do that' or to a community: 'Don't go that way!' and try to set myself up as if I were the Holy Spirit and start making a church to my liking, I would be quenching the Spirit.

But St Paul also tells me: 'Test everything and keep what is good'.

I pray very much to the Holy Spirit for that: the gift of discernment.

(*The Church is All of You. Thoughts of Archbishop Oscar Romero*, p. 62).

This prophetic function of discerning what God is doing within the community becomes increasingly important as the Church moves into a new way of working and relating. I found that the churches which were forging ahead with structural renewal had a strong sense of vision and vocation and that the leadership could articulate clearly what they believed that God was saying to them about their situation. Some had regular 'Open to God' Meetings, at which this process of discernment was being attempted communally, or a group that met to perform this function on behalf of the parish. But generally speaking the vision was coming from the leadership, particularly in those parishes which had the most holistic view of mission, though all of them had a core group in which this vision was being shared, tested and thought through. Where this vision was coming from the more gifted laity, and not being heard by the leadership, there was simmering discontent, and laity were taking themselves off and using their energies outside the parish, which was then seen as set over against what the whole business of spiritual renewal was about. Jean Vanier, founder of the L'Arche communities, devotes a whole chapter in his book *Community and Growth* to the gift of authority, and how it can be used in community to release the gifts of others. He says:

> One reason that people with responsibility fail to listen is that they fail to see the community as it really is. They become lazy optimists; 'Everything will sort itself out' becomes their slogan. Basically, they are frightened of acting, or feel incompetent in the face of reality. It is hard to be constantly conscious of reality, because it is disturbing. But it sharpens our awareness too. An aware authority is one which seeks to understand, prays and cries out to God. Its thirst for truth will grow and God will answer its cry. But at the same time, it has to be very patient, a true friend to time.
> (*Community and Growth*: Jean Vanier, p. 161).

One of the characteristics of the leadership in those churches that I visited which were becoming Stage 3 churches was the willingness to commit themselves long-term to the parish, and to work through the difficulties. One vicar said: 'I am a noisy upfront leader, but that is not what makes things happen here. What enables things to happen is that people trust me, they know that I won't take advantage of them, but for some of the people here that has taken a long time'. He had been in his parish for nine years; two of the clergy I interviewed had been in their parish for sixteen years. One of them said to me, 'The trust here is so great it frightens me. I feel that I could manipulate them so easily'. The other said, 'I don't need authority, I have it'. But this state of affairs had come after a long haul, after making mistakes and learning from them, meeting tensions and difficulties and seeing them as points of growth and learning, as pain barriers that have to be worked through in order that the community can be released to fulfil God's purpose for it. The confidence and courage to do this flowed from a strong sense of vocation to that community, from the experience of

117

spiritual renewal within it, and from a belief that God would honour their obedience to what they believed he was calling them to do. The problems only seemed to become destructive when that belief was shaken to the point where the leader failed to take a hurdle, became anxious, possessive or defensive, remained passive, or insulated himself from the warning signals that were around.

Renewing a church tests every aspect of leadership. It requires the ability on the part of the leader to stand pressure and tension, to handle conflict creatively and to be willing to endure aggression. 'I knew I would meet opposition', said a vicar, 'but I was surprised how much it hurt when it came'. But it is as the clergy show a lead in dying to status, to possessiveness, to a quiet life, that the lay awakening can begin to bring new life to the church community.

The willingness and ability of the leadership in the Stage 3 churches to spend themselves in order to release the giftedness of others showed itself in a flowering of all kinds of creativity within their communities. This was especially heartening to see in areas where there was a high level of unemployment, and few opportunities for creativity and expression within the secular environment. But the most striking characteristic of the communities that had weathered the storms and come through into both spiritual and structural renewal was their release into ministry and mission. Where the gifts of lay people had been released, even partially, the difference that this made within the community showed in a release of energy which overflowed into the environment. As the springs of spiritual renewal are increasingly tapped and channelled through the whole body of Christ, the perception of what the Trinity and the Christian community are doing changes yet again. The love relationship between the Trinity spills over into the church and

118

through it to the world not simply in theory, but in a communal experience of the renewing, healing, reconciling work of God. As the church members come into a right relationship with God, and with one another, they become increasingly open and giving towards the community and the environment around them.

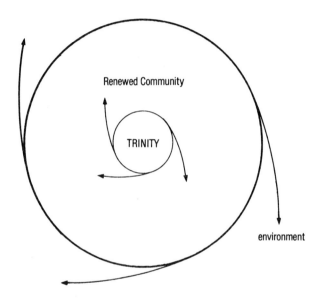

At this point there is a considerable amount of theological and structural convergence taking place between different kinds of renewed communities. I discovered four main avenues along which pioneers of structural as well as spiritual renewal were moving. As they begin to develop as a Stage 3 church, though they share the same basic concept of community, they each contain different elements and emphases. They are:

(a) *The Catholic Model*
The emergence of the lay apostolate, which restores the evangelical emphasis within Catholicism by encourag-

119

ing the priestly ministry of laity within their secular environment. The task of the clergy is to build the Christian community, the task of the laity is to Christianise their environment (The Cursillo Model).

(b) *The Evangelical Model*
This is at its most developed in Evangelical Charismatic parishes. The multi-cellular parish, which enables pastoral relationships to be extended through the church structure and beyond by the use of lay ministry, facilitates the full participation of all the members.

(c) *The Celtic Model*
Non-parochial communities which are linked through networks. These, as David Clark of the National Association of Christian Communities and Networks puts it, are communities of concern rather than place. They are centres to which people can come, or from which outreach can be attempted.

(d) *The Radical Model*
The building up of parishes and communities that are open to the wider community through centres of social concern.

These new structures, which are described more fully in Chapter 6, are much more open, lay-centred and mission-oriented than the pastoral parish structures that we have come to regard as the norm, and are better suited to the way we relate in today's society. I believe that in these models we are seeing the beginnings of an answer to some of our problems, although the process of discovery is still taking place, and we are still very much on the way. The Church is having to learn afresh, and in a radical way, what it means to be God's people today. And, like the experience of the Israelites in the desert, this learning process is coming about through conflict and difficulty, as well as through victory.

Archbishop Oscar Romero expressed this new emphasis succinctly:

> God wants to save us in people. He does not want to save us in isolation. And so today's Church more than ever is accentuating the idea of being a people.
>
> The Church therefore experiences conflicts, because it does not want a mass; it wants a people. A mass is a heap of persons, the drowsier the better, the more compliant the better.
>
> The Church rejects Communism's slander that it is the opium of the people. It has no intention of being the people's opium. Those that create drowsy masses are others.
>
> The Church wants to rouse men and women to the true meaning of being a people. A people is a community of persons where all co-operate for the common good.
> (*The Church is All of You. Thoughts of Archbishop Oscar Romero*)

The way we relate to one another in the Church is shifting, but we have not yet taken in the depth of the shift or the consequences that flow from it. The pioneers who have gone out in faith into uncharted waters have learnt valuable lessons which require deeper study and response from the whole Church. A sea-change is taking place in society both within and beyond the Church community. The greatest problem in our society has been diagnosed as loneliness; the greatest need is for fellowship. Next to 'Jesus in the heart', *koinonia* is the greatest gift that the Church has to give to people today. Spiritual and structural renewal are essential to the process of learning how to be God's people now, in the world and in the Church. Where I saw both being achieved, I saw the Church being renewed for mission.

121

DETAILS OF SOURCES QUOTED

'In Search of a Roundtable', Chuck Lathrop.

Community of Celebration Newsletter, September 1985: letter from Phil Bradshaw.

The Song of the Bird: Anthony de Mello. Image Books. Doubleday, New York, 1984.

One Inner Urban Church and Lay Ministry: Rev. Clarry Hendrickse. Grove Pastoral Series, No. 13. Grove Books, Bramcote, Notts, 1983.

The Open Church: Jürgen Moltmann. SCM Press, London, 1978.

The Church is All of You: Archbishop Oscar Romero. Collins Fount, London, 1985.

All Are Called—Towards a Theology of the Laity: CIO Publishing, London, 1985.

The Church in the Home: David Prior. Marshalls, London, 1983.

Community and Growth: Jean Vanier. Darton, Longman and Todd, London, 1979.

Enfolded in Love, Daily Readings with Julian of Norwich: Darton, Longman and Todd, London, 1980.

Chapter 6

RENEWAL AND MISSION

'The mission is where the renewal is'. The Diocesan Evangelist I had gone to see was emphatic about this. Spiritual renewal and mission, both in his individual life and in his overview of mission in the diocese, were inseparably intertwined. Everything I saw confirmed this statement. Also inseparably intertwined with spiritual renewal and mission was the Christian community, even among those who have tried to sit lightly to our structures, for each is part of a composite whole. The following extract from an essay on the spirituality of Cursillo endeavours to express the view of the connection between them. In it spirituality, ecclesiology and missiology go hand in hand:

> The mission of the Church is very original ... it is very urgent. But it is more easy to live it than to define it. The mission of the Church consists in extending in the world the life of Christ and in making mankind take part in the mysteries of the Incarnation and the Redemption. The mission, then, of the Church is that which establishes a communion of life with Jesus and a consequent communion of brothers among men. It is the mission of the Church to give birth to the Church, to make it live, to

123

spread it, to make it bear fruit in its own works of faith, of grace, and of the gospel message. As a living tree, the Church produces itself, produces its own branches, produces its own fruit. 'I am the vine, and you are the branches' says Jesus. In other words, the Church is an encounter with Christ and communion with brothers. (*Questions and Problems: Essay on the Spirituality of Cursillo*: Bishop Hervas).

That is a traditional view of the Church's mission. It might have been written at any time in the Church's history. What is new about it is the context in which it was written, for the Cursillo Movement seeks individual, community and society renewal, from a Church that has lost ground and finds itself in a post-Christendom situation.

The origins of our present parochial system lie in the agricultural, feudal society of early medieval times. The Celtic pattern of the gathered church, or monasterium, which supported more isolated mission churches, and which was characteristic of the Dark Ages, gave way in more settled times to mainly rural parishes, units of around 200 people, each with a parish priest, who was chaplain to the lord of the manor and his dependents. The psychologists tell us that 200 is about the number of people with whom we can manage to make a real relationship. Above that number, relationships become blurred and unsatisfactory. So it was the genius of the parochial system that it allocated one man to approximately the number that he could really get to know and care for. There was no need to build community in a village; it was already there. Everyone knew everyone else, and lived an integrated community life based on one industry (agriculture) which was largely self--supporting. But with growing urbanisation, this model of a parish, tailor-made to fit a rural society, became less and less appropriate to the new urban society with its totally different and more complex kind of belonging. As a result whole sections of the community have become unpastored and unchurched.

The Church today is reaping the harvest of centuries of structural immobility. How can it transfer the genius of the medieval parish to the twentieth century, but translate it in a way that makes sense in today's society? It has made itself totally dependent on its paid clergy, but their numbers are now a tiny handful compared with the huge numbers that need to be addressed. The traditional geographical parish has some (but only limited) relevance. People no longer live, work and relate totally within its boundaries. No matter how hard or how faithfully the clergy work, they can relate only to a tiny fraction of the population in an urban parish. In some city parishes clergy are touching only five per cent of the population, but are so busy that some of them are still under the illusion that they are ministering to the whole parish. 'We are a shrine for the neighbourhood' said one. 'I want to be in the Church of England because I want to minister to the whole community, not just a sect', said another. And as Donald Reeves, Vicar of St James', Piccadilly, said, 'We are trying to do something that is a sociological impossibility: to create community in a city full of strangers'.

In response to this situation other models have been emerging, both within and beyond the parochial system, that are closely linked to the experience of spiritual renewal.

a) The Catholic Model and the Cursillo Movement

In the 1940s, Roman Catholic theologians devised a strategy to meet the missionary task of the Church. They developed the idea of the apostolicity of the laity, which to them meant that the clergy were to continue to be the priesthood within the Church, serving the faithful remnant who remained. Lay people had an apostolic vocation, they were to be 'sent' as Christian witnesses to their own network of relationships and contacts in secular life. It was they who were called to fulfil the mission of the Church in the world. But though the theory, the strategy, the ecclesiology and the missiology were carefully worked through, in practice nothing very much seemed to be happening. The laity had become conditioned to passive dependence, and a re-orientation tantamount to a conversion was needed from both clergy and laity, before lay people could gain the confidence, vision and power to exercise their own priesthood in the wider community. Exhorting them to mission did not work. Law, not Gospel, had become the actual practice and experience of the Church, and while it kept a degree of order, it did not inspire most Christians in the pew to mission. It was not until the advent of the renewal movements that the theory of the lay apostolate began to spring to life in practice.

In 1948 some 70,000 young people, under the leadership of the Pilgrim Scouts of Spain, travelled to the shrine of St James to pray for the reconversion of Spain. They had got ready for the pilgrimage through workshops in which they studied the fundamentals of Christianity, and spiritually prepared themselves to be apostles of Christ. After the pilgrimage a three-day course was held in Majorca. Its chief purpose was to give to others the experience that many of those young people had had in their pilgrimage to the shrine of St James. This was the first of the three day Cursillos (Spanish for 'short course'), and from it the Cursillo Movement was born. The Cursillo is designed to 'unchain a Movement for Christian Renewal'. Christian Renewal in this context refers to the renewal of all society in a Christian way, achieved by living the life of grace. Cursillo does not aim to produce yet another church organisation or activity, but rather to utilise what is already there by bringing lay people to life through spiritual renewal, and through a rediscovery of what is fundamental to Christian living. Training and support are given to help Cursillistas to reach out to evangelise and Christianise their environment through the networks they already possess.

From its early beginnings in Spain the Movement spread, and Cursillos are now held all over the world. But when the direction of Cursillo was taken out of the hands of Eduardo Bonin and put under the control of Catholic Action, the result was that it became oriented towards renewing Church struc- tures. It has certainly had that effect (particularly in the Episcopal Church in the United States) but the Movement at present is trying to make its priority the originally intended task, the Christian renewal of society, and to recapture the 'environmental thrust' of its founders. Though Anglicans had made their Cursillos as guests of Roman Catholics before, the first joint Cursillo of Anglicans and Roman Catholics was held in 1968 in San Francisco. From then on Cursillo became an established method of renewal and mission in the Episcopal Church in the United States. Cursillo also takes place in the Lutheran, Methodist and other Churches.

In 1981 an Episcopalian group from Texas came to the Church in Wales and to the Gloucester Diocese, to start Cursillo there. Cursillo is growing in Wales and England; there are now two centres of Cursillo in Gloucester and Southwell Dioceses, and it is spreading into other Church of England dioceses.

Since Cursillo works through the Church structure, it cannot take place in a diocese without the consent of the bishop who is usually the first in the diocese to make the Cursillo. The next to come are the clergy. They then send the lay people whom they consider to be suitable. This helps to ensure that only those who are ready are sent on a Cursillo, and also that when they return to their parishes filled with enthusiasm, they are not frustrated by lack of support or understanding of their ministry from their parish and diocese. The Movement has been encountering some problems in this country stemming from a reluctance on the parts of bishops and clergy to identify with the Movement by coming themselves to Cursillo (though they are willing enough to send their lay people). Yet they themselves are an esential part of the process; Cursillo works through the structure, with the co-operation of the clergy and laity. Clergy need to have shared the experience that the lay people have been through so that they can help them forward when they get back into the parish again. The Cursillo weekend consists of an intensive three-day course, which combines teaching on the fundamentals of Christian living (all the things one should have been taught before confirmation but was not) together with preparation for leadership and witness. It provides a framework for an experience of spiritual renewal and of recommitment to the vows of baptism and confirmation; and it does this through close Christian fellowship, teaching and a great deal of prayer. The teaching stresses that we need to rely on God's power to do his will in us, combined with our faithfulness in prayer and participation in a full, sacramental life. Much training and preparation goes into the weekend, which is run by a lay Rector with a team of lay people and clergy, the clergy being responsible for spiritual direction. The management structure is interesting:

Lay Rector
(Chairperson, responsible for overall management)

Rector's Cha-Cha
(Administrative Assistant)
Spiritual Directors

(Counselling, vetting lay talks, giving some talks, administering sacraments)

Food Cha-Cha
(responsible for organising catering)

Music Cha-Cha
(responsible for all music)

Decuria Leaders
(Group leaders for the weekend.
Each gives one of the lay talks).

My experience of a Cursillo weekend was that it was even more liberating for the clergy taking part than for the lay people. There was a great deal of fun and laughter—one clergyman said, 'I haven't let my hair down like this since I was six years old'. He added, 'We have been talking about grace, experiencing grace, and living in God's grace the whole weekend'. Another said, 'I have learnt so much this weekend. I now have the courage to go back to my parish and set in motion the things I know I must do towards renewal'. After a doubtful start, one could see the lay participants coming to life and gaining in confidence and fellowship as we worked our way through the gruellingly intensive course. Messages arrived from all over the United States from Cursillistas who were praying for us over the weekend. Some parishes had organised a three-day vigil of prayer; some were praying with fasting.

In spite of some heartiness and emotional pressure which might have been counter-productive with

English people, the weekend worked. One lay person said, 'I have realised for the first time what being a disciple of Jesus really means'. The close fellowship that had built up during the weekend exploded into an exhibition of bearhugging at the Peace which would have made many a charismatic church look cold by comparison. It had been an experience of spiritual renewal for many of the participants and a source of encouragement to the staff who had worked so hard.

After the weekend (The Three Days) comes what is called the Fourth Day—the rest of one's life. Cursillistas are given a support-group, called an Ultreya to help them to work out in their lives what they have been taught at the weekend, and to have the grace to persevere. Their task is how to live, work and pray for the Christianising of their environment. They have been taught how to evangelise through their network of relationships. 'Be a friend, make a friend, bring that friend to your friend Jesus'. At the group reunions they report back regularly on what they have been doing to nourish themselves spiritually, what study they have been undertaking, and report success or disappointment in the apostolic action they have attempted. In addition two testimonies are given, one which stresses achievement, the other failure or frustration. The Cursillista is taught to expect failure as well as success (some people have always said 'no' to God) but failure is seen as an opportunity to learn and as a 'tempering of the apostle'. The clergy member present 'gospelises', i.e. he supplies some theological reflection on what has been said in the testimonies. By prayer, sacrament, study, and the help of a support-group the laity are encouraged to sustain their Christian life and its outreach.

It was clear from the Ultreyas or group reunions that I have attended since the weekend that the laity needed more ongoing teaching and encouragement in their apostolic mission, and that the clergy were essential to help in this confirming exercise, though they were not always present to do so. It is in the Ultreya that the acid test of the Cursillo method is experienced; whether it has indeed transformed the participants so that they can in their turn penetrate and transform their environment, or whether the group dwindles merely into a fellowship for those who have made their Cursillo.

A Commentary on the talks given at a Cursillo weekend says:

> The Cursillo Movement attempts to offer the Church and the world men and women who are formed in what is fundamental for being a Christian so that they will, in their own individual responsible way, and with initiative, infuse the gospel into all levels of society.
> (*The Three Days, A General Commentary on the Lay Talks of the Cursillo Weekend*).

Cursillo is a tried and tested method of focusing the elements of Christianity in order to motivate the laity into mission. Because of its origins it has a Catholic slant, and appeals particularly to Anglo-Catholics, although it has a strongly evangelistic emphasis and purpose. As it grows within the Church of England it will help the Anglo-Catholic parishes in particular to activate their lay people into mission. But, as we shall see, some within the Charismatic Movement would wish to take the idea of the apostolate further than this, to be the pioneers of new community. An unresolved question lies at the heart of this vision of the Church invigorated by an active lay apostolate that is engaged in the renewal of society. That question is: how do we understand the nature of the apostolate itself today?

In the New Testament the apostolate is not simply the outreaching arm of the Church; apostles are the founders of new communities. As they speak the word, Christian community is created, and a new Church is

131

born. The Acts of the Apostles give us example after example of this. When Christianity became established as a state religion, however, the need for this pioneering work dwindled, and the ministerial structure that had included apostles, prophets, pastors, evangelists and teachers gave way to a more settled way of life in which pastors and teachers were mainly required to give pastoral care to the community that was already there. This pastoral pattern and emphasis has been with us ever since.

We find ourselves today back in a missionary situation, back in the days of the apostolic communities. There is a need to break fresh ground; we need the apostolate again, not just for outreach, but to plant new communities. The Cursillo Movement represents a half-way house between a pastoral and a missionary Church. It restores the idea of the apostolate, but does not take it all the way; the full impact of our missionary situation has not been assimilated. It keeps the core within the present framework of a pastorally-oriented Church, where the function of the hierarchy is to teach, sanctify and govern, and the ordained priesthood has the task of building up the ecclesial community, which is rooted in the existing parish structure.

b) The Evangelical Model and the Charismatic Movement

John Wesley has disappeared into the dim distance of historical respectability, but he would have been very much at home with the 'goings-on' in the Central Hall, Westminster, at the Conference being held there by John Wimber and a team from his Church, the Vineyard Fellowship in the United States. An ecumenical group of Church leaders had packed every seat in the Hall for a week-long 'teach-in' on the ministry of healing under the title of the 'Third Wave'. What is the

'Third Wave', and why would John Wesley have felt at home with it?

There is at present an expectation in Charismatic circles that we are on the brink of a third contemporary movement of God's Spirit—the first being the Pentecostal Movement earlier in this century, which was rejected by the traditional Churches, but gave rise to the Pentecostal Churches. The second is seen to be the Charismatic Movement, which has brought about renewal within the denominations and also given rise to the House Church Movement. Interpretations of what this Third Wave is (or will be) vary from a belief that it will prepare the Church and the world for the Second Coming of Christ, to the more modest claim of John Wimber that it will bring a wider spectrum of Church people into the sphere of renewal.

The teaching at the Conference focused on the 'Signs and Wonders' depicted in the New Testament as an integral part of Jesus' ministry and mission, and on their meaning, the way in which they demonstrate the Kingdom of God. John Wimber, in explaining the purpose and method he uses in teaching about 'Signs and Wonders', may also be explaining the attraction that so many Evangelicals have felt towards the Charismatic Movement. He says in his book *Power Evangelism* (p. 107), 'Evangelicals emphasise knowledge about God through Bible Study. This produces a heavy emphasis on intellectual formation, but in the classroom situation, this can skew the goal of discipleship away from moral and spiritual formation.' He quotes Russel Spittler who says, 'The historical-critical method (of studying Scripture) is inadequate ... because it does not address piety'. Or, as John Wimber himself puts it, 'The student easily falls into reliance on study instead of reliance on the Holy Spirit'. He sees Christ on the other hand as being more action-oriented. As well as teaching his disciples, he trained them by showing them

133

what he did, and involving them in his action. John Wimber copies this method in teaching about the ministry of healing. During the session we had some straight teaching about 'Signs and Wonders' which 'show us what the Kingdom of God is like; (they) ... reveal glimpses of God's love, peace, joy'. There was also a time of worship, after which we were drawn into the healing activity of God's Spirit by being called to minister to one another, and by the Holy Spirit being called down upon us to initiate the training process. The orderly chaos that then broke out resembled the accounts of the Wesley meetings when he 'spoke the Word, and the Spirit fell upon the hearers'. Repentance and healing followed—mostly inner healing of the psyche. 'What do you think of this?', I asked a colleague. 'Marvellous in the hands of mature spiritual leaders', he said, 'I have never seen anything like the depth of repentance that is going on here, but in the wrong hands —disastrous'. Unlike the Wesley meetings, there was an Anglican bishop up on the platform taking part, and most of those present were mature spiritual leaders who were involved both in healing and in being healed.

But these occurrences are problematic for some. John Wimber says in his book, 'If Christians have a world-view that is affected by Western materialism, they will probably deny that signs and wonders are for today. Though they may use a theological rationale, the real issue is that it upsets their world-view. In contrast to this, a second group of Christians have a world-view that is affected by Western rationalism; they might acknowledge signs and wonders, but consign them to the irrational ... They do not understand the purpose of signs and wonders, to demonstrate the Kingdom of God'. For him, the miraculous events are 'trans-rational', that is, they transcend the secular world-view of modern rationalism, which, although it does not share the eighteenth-century rationalist view that it is possible to analyse all experience objectively, nevertheless tends to believe in a closed material universe under-stood only by scientific enquiry, while religious and moral matters are relative. John Wimber maintains that though they transcend this world-view, signs and wonders are nevertheless meaningful phenomena, which we should study and endeavour to understand. He accepts the supernatural events as being just that, but is nevertheless thinking hard about them. He is not content to remain agnostic. The Biblical account and his spiritual experience affirm his belief that there are two Kingdoms, the Kingdom of God and the Kingdom of Satan. These Kingdoms are in conflict, and Christians have been drafted into Christ's army to do battle against Satan. Evangelism is meant to go forward in the power of the Holy Spirit, as this battle is fought and won by Christians in the name of Christ. We are not cut off, as secular thinkers assume, from divine intervention; indeed, without it we cannot win the battle. He describes those who deny the signs and wonders related in the New Testament account as 'theological secularists, materialists cloaking their philosophy with religious language'.

John Wimber's work is having considerable influence among Evangelical Charismatics, who are the fastest-growing constituency in the Church of England today. His argument and its conclusion show both the Evangelical dilemma in reconciling the Biblical account with modern understanding, and also the new confidence that they feel in doing so. The Charismatic Movement satisfies their desire for a more holistic spiritual life, an integration of mind, heart and spirit in their discipleship, and also illuminates an area of spiritual phenomena described in the Bible, but requiring a new kind of understanding today. In his book there is also a new awareness of symbol and its meaning, something which the Evangelical has in the

135

past neglected. These three elements combined are a possible explanation of the tremendous influence of the Charismatic Movement on the Evangelical wing of the Church, and of its especially rapid growth there. The coming-to-life in spiritual renewal, and the coming-to-life of the Biblical account are linked, and resolve the difficulty of addressing the Bible as divine revelation, and of communicating this revelation to others in the light of our modern understanding and world-view. This resolution leads to a new confidence and vigour in evangelism and mission.

Evangelicals have also been concerned with style and structure. For those who wish to communicate with people outside the Churches today, the charismatic style of presentation is closer to the cultural context in which they are living, and Evangelicals who are not themselves card-carrying Charismatics have nevertheless adopted the vehicles of modern music, art and drama that the Charismatic Movement has produced. The practice of mounting 'Guest Services' to which outsiders can be invited, to experience a lively and accessible form of worship, has thus been given a fresh lease of life by the Charismatic style, and this method of drawing people into an informal atmosphere which is nevertheless deeply devout is an effective means of evangelism. There are generic similarities in structure too. The Bible Study group has for a long time been the staple of the Evangelical congregational structure. This can be a vehicle through which Spiritual Renewal (in whatever form) can percolate through into a parish. A diocesan missioner described the way in which Charismatic Renewal infiltrates a parish thus:

Phase 1: Individuals experience Charismatic Renewal.
Phase 2: Charismatic groups come together for worship, bible study and ministry of the gifts; the 'Wednesday night' phase.

Phase 3: The Charismatic Renewal begins to have an impact on the main structures of the parish—the Sunday worship, the congregational structure—'the painful phase'.

Phase 4: The whole community is renewed.

The distinctive structure of the Evangelical Churches extends the pastoral system within the Church, through the way in which the clergy share their ministry with the laity. A feature of this is the eldership group, which shares with the trained staff the day-to-day decision-making and running of the parish. But this basic concept functions in a variety of ways. Mark Birchall carried out a study of 158 churches with eldership schemes, and visited all of them, but found that each was as individual as a finger-print. I was able to visit a relatively small number, and my remarks stem from a less comprehensive and concentrated study. Nevertheless I found a family likeness as well as a variety in the different parishes that I visited. The core group, whether it was called an eldership, or whether it was a Standing Committee or an Executive Committee, was fulfilling a role on behalf of the Parochial Church Council alongside the staff team. It seemed to be very important for the working of this group that it should be elected by the Annual General Meeting, not just the Parochial Church Council (let alone nominated by the vicar), because otherwise there was a danger of its not representing the whole parish, and being seen to do so. Where the vicar had nominated his own group, there was a suspicion of it on the part of the Parochial Church Council, who were uneasy about its lack of relationship to them. It was also seen as important that the group's members should have real pastoral responsibility within the parish, rather than being nominated because they were people with ideas but with limited knowledge of how the parish operated internally or with a limited contact with other parishioners.

137

Spiritual Renewal causes an increase in lay activity within small groups, and (as will have been seen from Chapter 5) the oversight and support of these groups, while allowing them to function with some degree of freedom, is essential to healthy growth within the parish. Sunday worship is like the tip of an iceberg; for in such churches the greater part of the work is taking place in group activity during the week. The largest of the multi-celled churches that I visited had at the peak of its internal growth over a hundred Bible Study groups and eighty task groups. The structure that helps to build this growth is also a nurturing environment, suitable for new Christians who are attracted to the Church in the wake of Spiritual Renewal. One key reason for the growth of multi-celled parishes in renewal is their ability to attract and hold new Christians through this fellowship and structural support.

David Wasdell, in his paper *Long Range Planning and the Church*, sees the growth and management of cellular groups (found in their most highly developed form in the Evangelical Charismatic Churches) thus:

A. The unicellular structure: all the congregation relates personally to the vicar.

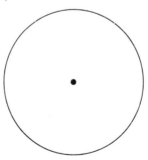

B. The vicar relates to the group leaders, who take pastoral charge of the group members. The vicar has

138

the role of episcope in the New Testament sense of the word, i.e. he is overseeing the (lay) pastors.

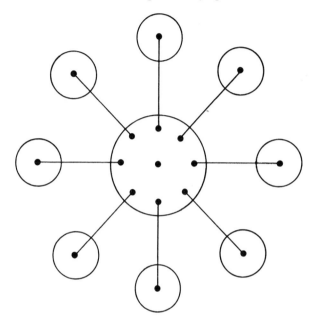

C. The group leaders relate to an intermediate group of leaders, either a member of the staff team, a Pastoral leadership group, or an elder.

Among the groups in the multi-celled parishes that I visited were task groups, some of which were engaged specifically in mission. Some parishes had lay evangelism groups, in which those lay people who were deemed to have the gift of evangelism operated together as a team. Some were employed as full-time evangelists, who co-ordinated the work of volunteers in the parish in the field of evangelism and mission. Others were more broadly missionary, and were engaged in social action or community work. One parish employed a full-time community worker, whose work

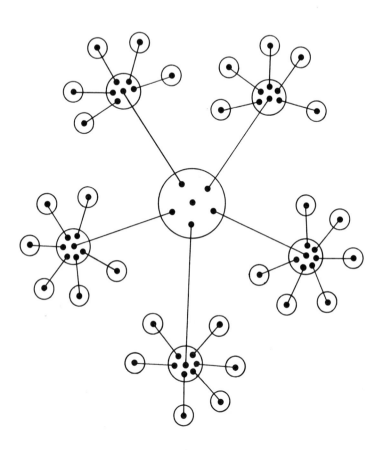

among young people had proved so successful that they claimed that all glue-sniffing and vandalism had disappeared from the parish. One full-time evangelist coordinated a group of volunteers who manned a kind of Citizens' Advice Bureau, where people could go for help. Another parish ran parish missions, in which teams of lay people with a clergy leader ran missions in other parishes who asked for help.

As a result of all these evangelistic and missionary efforts, by the time the church gets to Stage C in David Wasdell's projection, it is usually bursting the parochial seams in terms of congregational size. When the whole congregation comes together on Sundays, they have difficulty in squeezing into the main church building, and the size and complexity of the pastoral structure can put severe strain on the staffing levels. Finding and training enough leaders is a constant pressure on the existing leadership, as newcomers continue to crowd in onto an already overloaded pastoral structure. But even before the parish becomes overfull, it needs to be thinking about church planting.

Some churches are planting within their parish, building separate congregations on the 'strawberry runner' principle as offshoots of the mother plant, and using school halls or community centres as their place for the celebration level of worship. Others have planted (or are seeking to plant) outside their parish, since they have eclectic congregations drawn from a wide area. Here they run into difficulties, because they are then seen as in competition with already existing Church of England churches in the area or deanery. But to advise the cell groups and their members that they ought to attach themselves to their local Church of England church is to ignore the metamorphosis that has taken place in the whole structure of the eclectic church. It is no good telling a lay person or group in a Stage 3 church, which is engaging its laity in full

141

participation, to go back into a Stage 2 or possibly a Stage 1 church, where they are likely in isolation to experience afresh the frustration which may have led them to go to the Stage 3 church in the first place. One answer that has been tried, and seems to be working, is of planting some of the congregation from a Stage 3 church, with a Stage 3 leader, into a nearby parish church which is about to be made redundant and has little, if any, existing congregation. Where this has been done there has been a revival of the redundant parish, which tends to grow more slowly than the mother, but nevertheless takes root.

This type of multi-celled structure has enormous potential for growth, particularly when it is linked to a strong drive towards evangelism, because in today's climate there is a greater openness to the Gospel. It is primarily responsible for the fact that there are now many Evangelical and Evangelical Charismatic churches that are experiencing such problems of growth. Their situation is nearly incomprehensible to other parts of the Church which are struggling to survive, and the contrast is extreme. All the Evangelical churches I visited that were experiencing renewal, whether it was Charismatic Renewal or the lay awakening, were distinguished by a verve, vigour and vitality that was refreshing. But the rate of change and growth that they were experiencing can put a heavy strain on the leadership. The price of this renewal is that it brings the danger of 'burn-out' to those who are endeavouring to minister to the growing numbers. The influx of newcomers often means that the Church is full of immature Christians, who need to be helped to grow in their discipleship, and this takes much time and effort. The structure is there to help them, but the need for mature Christians to man it is often greater than the supply. One parish I visited was turning itself into a lay training centre, where approximately fifty lay leaders a year could be trained and commissioned, but it was still having difficulty in keeping pace with the demand. This effort to equip and train lay leadership goes alongside a rise in the number of vocations to the ordained ministry, although they are still not enough to offset the decline in other parts of the Church. From the two Evangelical theological colleges I visited, the staff at one of them estimated that 80 per cent of the ordinands had been affected by the Charismatic Movement, while at the other the staff said that most of them had been affected by it. The growth of the Evangelical (and particularly of the Evangelical Charismatic) Churches in congregational numbers, parishes, and numbers of ordinands, combined with the recent decline in other sectors of the Church, is bound to affect the constitution of the Church of England, as the impact of this growth begins to be felt beyond parish boundaries.

c) The Radical Model—a case study

Just say
You saw me.
You spoke to me.
You know I'm here.

Don't come back
And tell me
You forgot.

I matter
I'm a person
Though I may not be much.
Just a bundle of rags—
Held together by string.

I sleep
Under the railway arch
In a cardboard box,
And I live
On cider and gin.

143

It's no sort of life,
I know.
But it's that
To which I've grown used.
I don't feel the cold any more.

I can't last much longer.
I can feel that
In my bones
But that's why it's important
That someone knows
I'm here.
Because I'm a person
And I matter.

(Taken from *Prayer from a Searching Heart*: Ian Calvert, published and copyright 1985 by Darton, Longman and Todd and used by permission of the publishers).

A religious in a community that I visited told me of a vision that she had which had the nature of a dream. She was standing in the shell of a ruined church, and on the altar were three crosses. One was plain; one was rather ornate; the third was a crucifix, with a representation of the crucified Christ on it. She understood without being told (as one does in a dream) that the plain cross stood for Protestantism, the ornate cross for Orthodoxy, and the crucifix for the Roman Catholic Church. Between her and the altar sat a beggarman, holding out a box of matches, and she understood without being told (as one does in a dream) that he represented Everyman.

This vision, or waking dream, is full of allusion, and could be interpreted in a number of ways. But what is striking about its insight is that it is the opposite to triumphalist Christianity, or confident humanism. We have indeed come, according to this vision to the end of Renaissance man. Both humanity and the Church are portrayed as empty, needy. The Church is an empty ruined shell, Everyman is a down-and-out beggar (like the one Prebendary Ian Calvert was describing), a sign

144

of our spiritual poverty. Earthly glory has departed, and the three crosses reflect in their different ways a God whose glory is shown in dereliction. It is a picture of brokenness.

Can a Church, which is an empty shell of what it once was, respond to the need of Everyman? Or is the ruined Church itself a reflection of humanity come to the end of its resources, but left with the triple image of the dying God? Or is it that in this dereliction and brokenness, the Church and humanity are most open to the meaning of the Cross and the hope of a Resurrection that comes through the power of God not through human effort?

It brought to my mind another picture. Over the entrance to the Church Missionary Society headquarters in Waterloo Road is an inscription that reads 'Go ye into all the world and preach the Gospel to every creature'. Underneath is a free-standing foundation stone laid by Sir Kenneth Grubb. One day, going into work, I passed two vagrants sitting on the stone swigging beer. These vagrants haunted us at CMS, they often came in under the porch out of the rain, and a little old woman sometimes passed by on some regular errand, dragging all her worldly goods behind her in a box tied with string. We seemed to be too busily engaged in world mission to be concerned with the mission literally on our doorstep. Since then, I understand, CMS have started to support a parish worker in the Waterloo area—a place which, for the homeless who have dropped through the Welfare State net, is the end of the line in more ways than one.

'There can be no renewal of the Church for an holistic mission without the help of the poor', said Rene Padilla, a Latin American pastor, to a conference at Post Green. And it was indeed in the more deprived communities that I visited, and among those who are most dispossessed, broken and alienated in our society, that an holistic mission was to be found.

Nothing I had read or heard before had quite prepared me for what I found at a radical parish that I visited. I knew that it was an overspill estate, the sort of place where no one wants to live, but where people are dumped from inner-city clearance in the mistaken belief that their living conditions are being improved. Clergy had come and gone here in rapid succession. Until the present vicar and his wife came, no one had lasted more than two years. They had felt called to the place, committed themselves long-term to it, and have been there nine years.

The estate was built fifteen or more years ago, and the high-rise flats which formed its core had proved to be a total disaster and had to be abandoned. As a result of pressure from the community (including the Church), they were in process of being pulled down. When I arrived their gaunt, empty shells still towered over the rest of the estate, and the building like a biscuit box beneath them that proved to be the church seemed dwarfed and inadequate by comparison. But it was the flats that were crumbling, not the Church. They were eloquent symbols of human dereliction, a man-made urban desert of the spirit, a well-meaning but bureaucratic attempt at community renewal which had gone hideously wrong. Four thousand people had been put into these monstrous blocks, built at enormous expense, but built so badly that when it rained the water poured in through the joins in the building units. Economies had been made on all the things that might have made life tolerable, like adequate lifts and communal facilities of every kind. Instead, life there became a nightmare, with the inhabitants living in isolation among an ant-heap, in constant fear of the crime and violence that bred in them. Now the flats are on their way out, giving way to the more pleasant cottagey squares that will in future make up the bulk of the estate. There is much more in the way of communal facilities than there used to be. But there are still problems. The area is an unemployment blackspot—50 per cent of the congregation of the church and 80 per cent of the young people are unemployed. Yet in spite of this when I entered the church building I found a cheerful, relaxed atmosphere, and one of the first things I heard was a lyrical prayer of praise to God from an unemployed youngster, as a group of us prayed together before the morning service.

When the present vicar and his wife first came to the parish, there was a small congregation, most of whom left, either because 'the vicar wouldn't do what he was told', or because they were not interested in prayer and bible study, or because the newcomers were not charismatic enough. Although they are Evangelical Charismatic Radicals, they are more Radical than anything else. However, other people began to come in, ex-Anglicans, ex-Roman Catholics, ex-Pentecostals and new Christians. I asked one man whether he had been a Christian before he came to the Church; the answer was 'No, I was a right villain!' So many came in that the congregation grew too large for the original building, which had to be enlarged. This gave a wonderful opportunity not only for the restructuring of the church building, but of the church community. It was rebuilt along Radical lines, as a community centre for the whole area, open to all for a variety of activities seven days a week.

It has been rebuilt for multi-purpose use, and consists of a chapel, a drop-in centre with kitchen, and a hall which is used for various activities during the week, but converts into a church on Sundays. There is also a bookshop, workshop, and offices from which to administer the MSC (Manpower Services Commission) scheme which the church is running. At the time of my visit the MSC scheme was employing nine people in the centre, who were helped by fifty-five volunteers. The staff consisted of the Scheme supervisor and a maintenance worker at the centre who also managed the training workshop, which taught skills in joinery, plumbing and electrics. The gardener who was maintaining the grounds was also setting up allotments for community use. The scheme secretary was also a bookkeeper and responsible for all the wages. A community worker was helping particularly with local pensioners and the 'mums' of the area, giving all sorts of practical help. The bookshop assistant purchased books from the Scripture Union to sell to local schools, and had been a great success. Two youth aides worked with children and young people, putting on suitable activities for them at the Centre. Another worked as a secretary to the Team Vicar. Volunteers manned the kitchen for the drop-in centre, and were responsible for other activities based there. 'There is so much to do, that unemployment is a nonsense', said the vicar. At the time of my visits, the parish was looking to double the size of the MSC scheme so that they could offer services to the housebound—the elderly and the disabled—as well as to those who were able to come to the centre.

How did spiritual renewal affect all this? What part did it play in building up the present community?

The vicar and his wife saw the 'upper-room experience' as something that they wanted to share with other people, although they wanted to be 'in the world'. The vicar believed that the balance between radical activism and the upper-room experience came from teaching the whole Bible, asking the following questions:

What is the nature of God?
What is his intention for the world?
How does all that impinge upon me?
What ought I to be doing in response to it?

The response as he understood it was a total apostolic ministry that involved the whole community. He saw the whole of the activity of the parish as a movement between the renewed worship of God, engaging the needs of the community, and the work of God that was communicated through the fellowship of his people. Social service and political activism without God's power quickly ran out of steam. Fellowship on its own could become merely a club, or a Christian ghetto. A high Charismatic 'trip' on its own could be undermining. But the healthy creative tension within the parish came from the interaction between renewed worship, Christian fellowship, and mission. They themselves found renewal in worship; they took regular days off to rest and to pray, or otherwise they found that they rapidly ran out of steam. But the reality of their worship came 'out of also being real in God's world'. Relationships were important, because progress took place as confrontation occurred, without pretence or collusion.

For example, when they first came, only six people came to Evensong. When it was discovered that the six were only coming to support the vicar, it was decided to close it down. As a result of Spiritual Renewal however a group of people wanted to pray. They came to the vicar's study to start with; then the group got too big for that, and met in a corner of the church. About a dozen came to this at first, but then the home groups started to come, and the prayer group grew to the size of a congregation; so the Sunday Service was restarted. People then really wanted to come to pray, instead of doing something unthinkingly when the original rationale for it had gone.

The vicar pinpointed four landmarks in the life of the parish that had raised people's sights, had increased their faith and their vision, and had made the parish grow spiritually.

The first was when they started to take seriously the calling of the church to serve the community. This did not happen until they saw the way in which the church building (rebuilt as a community centre) was actually working. The vision of a radical church serving the needs of the community came from the vicar, but the parishioners did not understand it until they saw the way in which the building was operating both as a focus and as a fulfilment of these needs. The influence that this vision had in the congregation was reflected in the ex-Pentecostal lay reader, who, when he joined the church, could not get to grips with community action at all, but who at the time of my visit (in addition to being put forward as a Non-Stipendiary Minister) was considering becoming a local candidate for Parliament.

An important lesson that the parishioners had learnt from the success of the new church building was that it was possible to take new initiatives; that it was possible to dream dreams and to see them fulfilled. This was especially significant for people who had exercised very little choice over the way in which their lives had developed, and who were used to being swept along by forces over which they felt they had no control.

A second factor which raised people's sights was attending a lay diocesan conference every year. Those church members who took part became aware that they belonged to a wider Catholic Church, and that to be a Christian cuts across culture, class, and national boundaries.

The third influence came through taking groups away from the parish to experience a renewed form of worship elsewhere. The response to going to a theological college's worship was, 'Wasn't that great! But it could never happen here'. Nevertheless decisions in the Parochial Church Council were influenced by their knowledge of what worship could be like.

The fourth landmark was a parish weekend. While

they were away together, quite unexpectedly, during a recreation period when they were relaxing, the Holy Spirit had fallen on their gathering and some miraculous healing had taken place. One woman told me of her healing from cancer of the throat, which had been vouched for medically. Others had experienced inner healing which showed in a new wholeness of personality. The vicar saw this unheralded event as being God's blessing on them because the parish was being faithful in mission. They had started with Radical Renewal, and had ended up with 'Signs and Wonders' but on the inside they just saw themselves as responding to God in the situation.

A more ongoing form of healing was taking place in the groups of young people, and also of wives, being ministered to by the vicar's wife. Members of a young people's group that I attended were able to share the more painful memories of childhood in a therapeutic way with one another, and to help each other to work through the adolescent difficulties that they were facing. Members of a wives' group were also able to help one another in their marriage problems. About 10 per cent of them had been sexually abused as children; others had been brought up in such an oppressive fashion that they found adjustment to married life difficult. Bible Study on God's purpose for marriage, together with the sharing of their difficulties within the group, was opening the way for healing to take place.

Some still found it hard to believe that God could and would accept them, because of things that had happened in the past; but others had come through from instability, irresponsibility and loneliness, to stability, relationship and greater peace with God and with themselves. The staff team saw the liturgical, healing ministry within the church as a continuous process of realising that God loves us and wants us to be whole. There was also a sense in which every service could be a healing service, because it was offering the opportunity of restoration to people, many of whom had a low self-image, and were very deeply wounded.

There had been some problems in establishing house groups in the parish, because the leaders lacked confidence and tended to give up when they encountered difficulties. They were introducing prayer triplets in order to get people together in small groups again. The parish was led by an eldership group elected by the whole church, but the vicar felt that the group was too small, and that more people should be involved in the decision-making.

The vicar believed that leadership was corporate; one did not have to distance oneself from parishioners in order to lead. On the contrary, it was as he became vulnerable to them that he gained their support. He had never been lonely, or stuck over decisions; there had always been some people in the parish with the insight he needed. They had made mistakes and wrong decisions, but they had learnt from them. They were inclined to be tentative in ministry, to try things out and see whether God blessed them. The leadership vision was renewed through allowing time for withdrawal and reflection, and through an openness to the wider Church. There needed to be space to think creatively. About his own leadership the vicar said:

> The only reason I retain leadership here is because folks trust me. When folks become more able they 'try it on'. There is a root of sin in all of us and we all like to push the boundaries. Any clergyman needs to be transparent as a person and honest about his own sinfulness, and needs to believe with all his heart that God has put him in that place for a particular purpose. It doesn't matter what kind of place or situation. You win your spurs, and people don't follow you until they feel comfortable with you, and feel that you can be trusted. For some people here that has taken a very long time. I am a noisy upfront leader, but that isn't what makes things happen here. It is because

people here have come to trust my judgement, and to feel that I will not abuse them. Being able to say 'sorry' is a great asset. People's attitudes are not fixed—you can change that. The keys are in the hands of the clergy in what they teach their lay people.

The parish asks for a very high level of commitment, but leaves it to the individual to work out what this means. Tithing, both of time, talents and money is a norm for the parish. The members of the congregation are given a booklet every year which lists jobs that need to be done, and parishioners are invited to volunteer for what they feel to be appropriate for them. This high level of commitment could set up a resistance in the 'envelope' of people in looser contact with the church, but this church was so open and giving to the community through the Community Centre that they had no difficulty in filling a coach every night for a week with non-Christians who wanted to go to 'Mission England' meetings. Of those who went, seventy-four went forward and made a commitment. The parish had useful contact with about sixty of these, of whom forty have since stayed on as regular members of the congregation.

The staff team felt that there was a growing commitment to God and what he wanted among people in the parish, but that this 'yo-yoed' according to where people were in terms of obedience. When the flats were emptied before being demolished a lot of the congregation was lost, but it was building up again. The community centre attracted people—fringe people were becoming members of the church, and new fringe people were appearing. The manager of the MSC scheme, a non-Christian, said, 'People found it difficult to believe that this is a church when I tell them what is happening here'. He explained, 'Churches are usually only concerned about themselves and their own congregations. But this church is caring for the whole

153

community without thought of return'. Or, as the vicar's wife put it, 'Whatever God is giving to us, we must give away'.

Here, among some of the most materially and socially deprived people in our society, I found a restoring, reconciling, healing Christian community that was touching and reforming the wider community around it. Morale was going up, not just in the parish, but in the area itself, which was being transformed from being a dumping-ground for alienated people, to being a place where people were able to find God, and community, and live.

d) *The Celtic Model*

Mission is God's mission, and God's activity is not confined to the Church, but related to the world ... I am an evangelist on the frontiers of the Church, but I have misgivings about putting the Church first—if one waited around for the Church to be right one would wait around for ever. The traditional Church is dreary and clergy-dominated—renewal makes it more lively and joyful, but it seems to be stopping at the renewal of the Church. I am interested in the renewal of the whole community and of the world. I can do without what happens in Church on Sundays, but I cannot do without worship, I cannot do without Christian fellowship, and I am renewed on Monday mornings. God speaks to me through ordinary people on the shop floor ... The lay apostolate liberates the Church—they are called by God to be in their job, and in it to experience the saving grace of God in their lives. Work needs to be taken seriously in the Christian context.

That is an Industrial Missioner speaking, a Charismatic Radical who is feeding back his Industrial Mission insights into the Church structure, but who is chiefly concerned with addressing the world of work with the insights of the Gospel. This means moving into a new theological dimension, but he finds much present

Charismatic theology superficial and conservative. His Evangelical origins take him back to the Bible as a quarry from which to build a new theology, which reflects on the experience of work in order to help to liberate the world of work. For example, like the Church, the world of work is inhibited by hierarchical ways of operating, which are effective in the short-term in carrying out an immediate task, but inhibit creativity and the entrepreneurial spirit, because they cannot thrive in those repressive conditions. On the other hand the ecumenical Industrial Mission team which he led was a coalition which had grouped itself around a common task, and worked in a much more informal and corporate manner. They shared their experience, reflected on it theologically, and then reached new theological understandings, new response and new practice (see Segundo circle, above). 'Analysis helps you to look more closely at a situation, but you can only get to a certain level with it. How does new vision come? In the Bible it comes not just through the "professional" prophets, it comes through "outsiders" like the Syro-Phoenician woman, the Good Samaritan, lepers, shepherds. God reveals himself through ordinary events and ordinary people, while we tend to be either super-spiritual or sub-spiritual'. He saw the creation of wealth as part of God's plan for the world, and the present industrial crisis as God's judgement on our institutions. But he also felt there was a renewed vision and hope in Christian circles.

Industrial Mission is one of many Christian groupings on the frontiers of Church life which focus on a common task. It belongs to what I would describe as the Celtic Model of the Church—that is, it consists of a gathered group from which outreach can be attempted, or to which people can come, but which is not rooted in the parochial structure—communities of concern rather than place, though located within a

155

network of relationships, based in this case on work. Like the renewalists within the parochial structure, most of the participants in the Celtic model of the Church are impatient with traditional structures, and have been exploring new ways of relating to one another, both within their Christian fellowship and in the wider community with which they are engaged. Spiritual renewal seems to have produced some of its most lively offshoots here, at the fringe of the Church's structure, unencumbered by traditional ways of working, and attractive to those who wish to be free of what David Clark in his book *The Liberation of the Church* sees as the bugbears of the 'captive church' and its closed structures—clericalism (though most of the leaders are in fact clergy), parochialism and congregationalism (though they are concerned with Christian community structures) and denominationalism (there is a high degree of ecumenism among the groups).

In medieval times the religious communities were responsible for education, mission and welfare. When they were abolished at the Reformation, the intention of the Reformers was to subsume their function within the new ecclesiastical structures; but as good Renaissance men, they tended to major on education, while mission and welfare were neglected. These gaps in the structure were filled from the eighteenth century onwards with entrepreneurial efforts by individuals and groups chiefly in the wake of such movements as the Missionary Movement, which produced voluntary societies responsible for mission and welfare, and the Anglo-Catholic Movement, which replaced the religious communities. Many of these older groups are now looking back to the original wishes of their founders, and are seeking to re-interpret them and their own vocation in terms of today's needs. Today's renewal movements have produced many more groups, but of a somewhat different style to their predecessors.

156

Extra-parochial communities seem to be grouped in two rings around the traditional church structure. There is an inner ring which is more closely related to the parochial church, and which contributes to the life of the parishes. Retreat and conference centres, for example, provide places to which people from the parishes can come. They have grown in number in response to the Retreat and Meditation Movements, which have had the effect of greatly increasing their use. Charismatic Renewal has also produced centres to which individuals or parishes can come for support and teaching. Religious communities have a distinct life and work of their own, but they too have increasingly opened their doors to those who are seeking an element of withdrawal and spiritual refreshment, and most of them now have guest-houses at which visitors can stay. A great number of voluntary societies now perform tasks with the support of people in the parishes, or offer services to them. An outer ring of task groups are working on the frontiers, and are concerned chiefly with the renewal of society, such as Industrial Mission, or Church Action with the Unemployed.

The rationale of the Celtic Church as a model for the Church today was explained to me by the Rev. Graham Pulkingham, the founder of the Community of Cele-bration. He had started the Community as a response to the need for lay training in the Church. It was an exploration into what it means to be a lay person fully committed to the Gospel in terms of today's living. The Community had felt the need for an element of withdrawal, in order to rediscover their Christian identity. Ordinary parish life was too immersed in the secular, which tended to overlay the Church's true identity and purpose. The Celtic model of the gathered Church, or monasterium, which acted as a transformer to generate new Christian activity and initiatives, and which supported missionary itinerants or mission cells,

157

was an appropriate model for them, and would increasingly become appropriate for others as we enter a new Dark Ages, a period where society is in a state of too much upheaval and transience to support a more settled form of Church.

Unlike the traditional form of religious community, however, this community was provisional; that is, people came in for long or short periods of time, but did not necessarily commit themselves to it for life. They contributed their possessions, they had everything in common, but they did not take vows of celibacy. Indeed at one period one-third of the Community consisted of children, because so many of their members were young married couples with families.

The Community was born in the 1960s in Houston, Texas, and was deeply influenced both by the Jesus Movement and by the Charismatic Movement. It came out of parish renewal, in a deprived down-town area. The original parish collapsed, but a group of people experiencing spiritual renewal stayed together, and from their life and ministry the core of the new parish developed. Graham Pulkingham saw the effect of the life of the Community upon those who moved in to the parish as bringing them from brokenness to healing, to wholeness and maturity, and then into leadership. He saw it as an inverted cone (see p. 159).

The Community moved to this country in the 1970s, and their parish mission teams (particularly the Fisher-folk) have had a profound influence on the growth and style of Charismatic Renewal in Church of England parishes. They still produce worship and teaching material for parish use, but as readers of their *Grassroots* magazine will realise, the thrust of their thinking has been shifting from being concerned with the renewal of the Church to being chiefly concerned with the renewal of society. They have become a

Growth of individual

Impact of community on individual

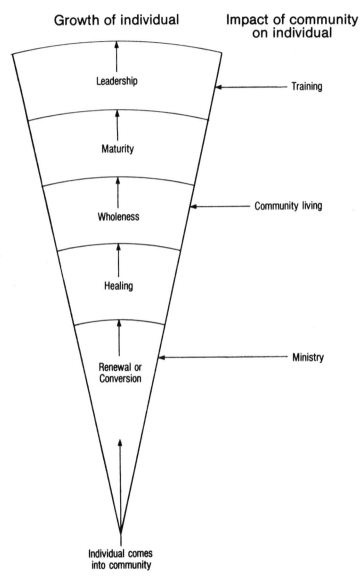

Leadership

Training

Maturity

Wholeness

Community living

Healing

Renewal or
Conversion

Ministry

Individual comes
into community

159

Radical community with a capital 'R', concerned with issues of peace and justice. They have now separated from the Post Green Community, which is concerned with pastoral work, and inner healing in particular. Some of them have gone back to the United States with Graham Pulkingham, others are moving to London.

Before they moved, I went to a conference held by the Community at Post Green. It was called 'The Way Forward for the Church'. Rene Padilla, a pastor from Latin America, who was the guest speaker, was advocating both Radical Renewal (that is, in this context, a renewal that is primarily concerned with issues of justice and peace) and the practice of basic Christian communities as experienced in Latin America. Our society is very different from that in Latin America; nevertheless there is now what David Clark calls 'the basic Christian community movement' in this country, analogous to the Latin American movement, which has been seeking to learn from its insights and to see how far the Latin American experience is relevant to the situation in this country.

These small communities of faith, or basic Christian groups (according to David Clark) 'offer the means of liberating a church in captivity and of achieving a communal breakthrough for church and world alike' (*The Liberation of the Church*, p. 73). Throughout the ages small groups have brought about reformation in the Church, and have addressed the crises of their own times in society. He analyses the stages through which they seem to have moved thus:

(1) *Protest*—against institutional rigidity or deviation in Church or society.

(2) *Withdrawal and dispersal*—the groups distance themselves from the main body, usually because of hostility from an authority which feels threatened by the new development.

160

(3) *Networking*—the coming-together through networking of the basic Christian groups.

(4) *Clarifying the message*—a time of reflection and self-examination.

(5) *Re-entry and re-engagement*—if the new development is not to become sectarian, it must offer its insights to the parent community.

(6) *Assimilation*—the new insights are taken into the wider system of Church and society. There remains a danger that institutionalisation will in time bring back rigidity and the need for further reformation.

(Most of the groups I visited were engaged in 3, 4 or 5; assimilation by the parent body has yet to take place, though it is beginning to happen in some areas of the Church's life).

The belief of some of those who are engaged in basic Christian groups is that spiritual renewal in small groups will bring about community renewal in both Church and society, through a grass-roots reformation. Rosemary Haughton, an English Roman Catholic, has said that she believes that these 'new little Churches and pre-churches are the spiritual future of the world'.

Whether this is too grand a view or not, it is clear that these groups have a significance out of all proportion to their size and number. They are proving-grounds in which the seeds of a new society are being tested out. The shift of the renewed parts of the Church towards a more lay-centred, ecumenical and missionary enterprise is to be seen at its most developed among them, and it was in these groups that I found the assumptions of present-day Church and society most vigorously challenged.

When I discussed these four models of Church with clergy at a Renewal day, one of them commented that we need elements of all of them in a parish—the emphasis on the lay apostolate of the Cursillo model, the small group structure of the Evangelical model, the openness to the community of the Radical model, and the networking of relationships and tasks of the Celtic model. That is certainly true, but in practice clergy often seem to be building one model only. In fact, if they are put in charge of another model of Church they will demolish it and build their own. This has not been fully recognised by dioceses who are not always sufficiently conversant with the new models and nuances of churchmanship. I came across a case of a Radical model of Church that had been demolished by Evangelicals, and a Stage 3 church (as described on p. 95) that had been demolished by a Stage 1 leader who had even persuaded the bishop to cancel the authorisation of lay pastors who had previously been commissioned by him! Dioceses are not likely to be confused by the differences between an Anglo-Catholic and an Evangelical, but it has not been sufficiently recognised that an Evangelical Charismatic Radical will be nearer to an Anglo-Catholic Radical than to a traditional Evangelical. Like the Anglo-Catholic Radical, he will build a Radical model of Church, whereas the traditional Evangelical will build the Evangelical model. When it comes to the differences between Stages 1, 2 and 3 (above), dioceses should recognise that it takes at least two years for the clergy leader of a parish to make the transition between the stages, and that a Stage 1 leader will not instantly be able to cope with the delegation required and the complexity of structure of a Stage 3 church. The effect on the parish of being built, demolished, and then rebuilt can be traumatic, and great care is needed to ensure that the person who takes over a renewed parish can cope with the new model. The more advanced and complex the structure, the more advanced the leadership skills need to be. Fortunately such skills can be learnt, and there are now clergy who can give the retraining that is necessary. More and more clergy are going to need this retraining as the rate of change takes them rapidly beyond what they were originally trained to do.

One of the primary lessons to be learned is that those responsible for clergy appointments should be aware of the issues considered in this chapter. Where there are a number of parishes engaged in renewal, a diocesan strategy will become necessary, and a training programme for clergy, as well as for lay people.

DETAILS OF SOURCES QUOTED

Questions and Problems: Essay on the Spirituality of Cursillo: Bishop Hervas. Ultreya publications, Dallas.

The Three Days, A General Commentary on the Lay Talks of the Cursillo Weekend: National Ultreya Publications, Box 210 226, Dallas, Texas 75211, 1984.

Power Evangelism: John Wimber. Hodder and Stoughton, London, 1985.

Long Range Planning and the Church: David Wasdell. Urban Church Project.

Prayer from a Searching Heart: Ian Calvert. Darton, Longman and Todd, London, 1985.

The Liberation of the Church: David Clark. NACCAN, Birmingham, 1984.

Chapter 7

LIVING WORSHIP

The search for a renewed form of corporate worship in the Church of England has been going on for most of this century, and reached a climax in the publication of the Alternative Service Book in 1980. After the abortive attempt to introduce the 1928 Prayer Book, the Church returned in the 1960s to a period of experimentation, after which it attempted this great leap forward, one of the most ambitious attempts at institutional renewal in its recent history. The new Alternative Service Book is not just a translation of the old liturgy into modern English; it incorporates a modern understanding of the corporate nature of the Church and of its priesthood. The Church is seen not only as the place where we encounter God, but also as the place where we encounter one another. The priesthood of all believers is exercised corporately by the whole congregation, and the priest becomes the president, representing the congregation. Doctrinal understandings have shifted—there is more emphasis on resurrection and ascension. Everlasting life—the life beyond the grave—becomes eternal life, the new life of God that we receive through the Holy Spirit, a present reality, not only for the future. There is an absence of references to the anger and judgement of God; we sin through ignorance and weakness, as well as through our own fault. A shift in attitudes is reflected in the liturgy which is still in the process of working its way through into the consciousness of the Church as a whole.

On Advent Sunday, 1984, I was visiting a northern diocese, and went to two services which perfectly illustrate the shift that has been taking place in the way we worship.

In the morning I went to a city church. On entering I was handed a couple of books without comment, and went to find myself a place in the pews, where the congregation seemed to be scattering themselves so as to be as far away from one another and from the scene of action as possible. An immaculately staged and beautifully sung service followed, in which the emphasis was exclusively on the otherness of God. In fact it felt, as I sat in the lonely isolation of my pew, as if I was putting in a long-distance telephone call to a God who was somewhere in outer space, so far away was the act of worship taking place at the high altar, and so inaccessible did the God we were attempting to worship seem to be. The sermon was about the long dark tunnel that we were going through in this life, a darkness lit only by the flickering candle of Christian hope which we carried. We would emerge from the end of the tunnel one day into the light of Christ in the next life. Meanwhile the message of Advent was that the light was there at the end of the tunnel somewhere! And with this assurance I left, not having communicated with a soul.

In the evening, I went to a service in a church in a mining town nearby. I was greeted warmly by three people before I had scarcely crossed the threshold, and shown to a seat in a packed church where everyone was chattering to one another in an animated fashion. The grey Norman pillars were hung with colourful banners, pronouncing 'Jesus is King' and the 'Fruits of the Spirit'. Instead of a surpliced choir there was a music group, who competed bravely with the chattering congregation in an attempt to introduce a worshipful atmosphere. It was difficult to shut the congregation up in order for the service to begin. The theme of the service was 'Christ, the light of the world', and the emphasis was on the immanence of God. In the sermon we were told that the light of Christ was here, now, and that all we had to do to pass from the darkness of sin into his light was to surrender our lives in penitence and faith to him, to make a commitment to him, and the light of Christ would enter our lives. A drama group illustrated the theme vividly in mime, and then as we sang 'The light of Christ has come into the world', there was a sense of the presence of God within the congregation that engaged us in real worship. After the service there was coffee, and more greeting. The fellowship within the congregation reached out and welcomed the outsider into its life.

These two services represent two extreme polarities; most churches are somewhere in between. The first service was reminiscent of the anonymous kind of worship in which most people aged over forty in the Church of England have been brought up. What has been emerging in the Church as a whole, through spiritual and liturgical renewal, has been the corporate experience of God expressed in *koinonia*. 'God with us' is at the core of the renewal—i.e. the corporate experience of the immanence of God which is expressed in living worship and grasped in our relationship to our neighbour.

There is also a reaction to an English cultural imbalance (our denial of emotion), particularly among young people. There is a shift of consciousness, an attempt at emotional integration. The Charismatic Movement has had a very significant impact, particu-

167

larly on student groups—the style of their meetings has become more spontaneous, more informal; there is more singing, more joy, but there is less intercession and confession, and a shrinking from the shadow side of life. Some students who are not Charismatic are going to Charismatic churches because of the ethos. A new kind of Anglicanism and Puritanism is emerging in the Christian groups—a shift from individualism to seeking community, and from repression to expression. There are occasional excesses, but these are not general; the majority are getting on with living the Christian life, and Christian societies working among students find the situation generally very encouraging.

This greater openness, particularly in the expression of devotion to the person of Jesus, rather than in repression of it, comes as a great relief to some older people, but is genuinely shocking to others. A diocesan bishop said to me, 'It is so wonderful that we can talk to each other about how we relate to Jesus'. Others, brought up to believe that one must never show even the most spiritual of emotions, or share the deeper side of one's nature, find this hard to take. Brought up to despise emotion, they tend to dismiss it as superficial or lightweight. They are used to repressing this side of themselves, which in recent English culture was suppressed but which re-emerged in a highly disguised and ritualised form. What Yehudi Menuhin (describing Elgar) called 'The poetic heart behind the English tweed' used to be a cause of grave embarrassment, a positively 'no-go' area. It found religious expression in the highly individual communing with God of the eight o'clock spirituality, and in the poetic, Tudor language of the Book of Common Prayer, which gives a strong sense of the numinous. Some of those brought up to this introvert way recoil from a more extrovert style of worship and relationship which asks them to relate to God and their neighbour in an open manner. Much of the difficulty that liturgical renewal has encountered is due to this cultural shift, the depth and extent of which has been little understood on both sides of the renewal fence. It is not just a case, as advocates of liturgical reform have tended to say, of bringing the language of our services up to date so that they are 'understanded of the people'. In order to put into practice modern theological insights into the nature of worship and community, we have been asking people to come out from behind social fences where many of them have been living all their lives. This is asking a great deal, and it does not take into account the reasons why the social and emotional distancing is there in the first place, nor the attempt of the community to deal with and contain parts of human nature which could constitute a threat to equilibrium. The stoical way of salvation expressed in the first Advent service that I went to is aimed at enabling one to persevere through the difficulties and pain of life, without giving up or surrendering to the emotion of the moment. Social distancing is a protective screen, which in the religious context is used to produce an inner recollection and communion with God, an attention to things spiritual. But it is done at a cost. It makes any kind of real community impossible; the suppression of participation and feeling has a deadening effect; the rigid containment can take away challenge and cutting edge, leaving the personality locked in.

> The stoic avoids the ravages and abyss of shame at the cost of the possibility of joy. His world is marked by order and imperturbability in face of disorder, but he misses what we have called the reality of the overflow. A God of joy is inconceivable as ultimate reality, and the feasting, dancing and endless praise seems dangerously escapist, threatening his equilibrium. He has attained an eminently sensible solution, which is by no means easy, and all his energy is taken in keeping to it. (*Jubilate—Theology in Praise*: Daniel W. Hardy and David E. Ford, p. 95).

169

An opening to greater joy brings with it the risk of greater pain and vulnerability. As Lawrence Hoyle of Anglican Renewal Ministries says, 'The cross is at the heart of renewal. *Agape* (love) means a vulnerability to suffering. There is a black hole in the middle of cloud nine'.

But the extent of the inhibitions that our social conditioning has produced can be seen in churches that have been engaged in renewal for a number of years now, where there are still people who cannot bring themselves to turn to their neighbour and shake hands in the Peace. Their sense of private space is violated by attempts to coerce the congregation into a consciousness of their participation with other members, if not into true community. The inner recollection they have learnt to cultivate is shattered by the distraction of having to look outwards.

Pax

I shall not go to Church again,
They gave the peace you see.
My neighbour put his hands on mine
And spoke to me.
I do not care for that.

Many years have passed
Since I was touched, save by the priest's hand,
Dismissing me.
I do not care for it. I do not care for it.
I have always kept myself to myself.
My neighbour put his hands on mine
And spoke to me.

I do not know now, how I could turn,
Place my own hands upon another's
And speak to him;
But this I did
Impelled by the Peace.

... The Peace, the priest said;
Is this then, peace?
This broken shattered self that cries within?
I have had to touch my neighbour
And he touched me,
I shall not go again.
But he was Christ
Who stood on either side of me.
(*Step into Joy*: Joan Brockelsby).

'Where can I go?' wrote one woman to a newspaper, 'to escape the handshaking and the choruses?' 'It expressed a togetherness that I did not feel' commented a clergyman on the renewal-type worship he had experienced at a conference. The attempt to impose a more corporate style of worship can make some people feel more alienated.

Others welcome the friendlier, more relaxed atmosphere of worship. At one parish I visited in a very deprived area, the vicar told me that he sensed that the hugging that went on during the Peace was very important for some of his congregation. It said, 'God loves you, the Church accepts you, you are important to us'. Social distancing is not just the product of the stiff-upper-lip public school, it goes right through our society. The vicar's wife told me that her working-class background had conditioned her not to touch: 'My father never touched us except to wallop us'; she felt that physical touching was an important way of breaking down a wall of indifference with which many of the congregation, like her, had been surrounded since childhood.

But renewal in corporate worship is not just concerned with breaking down the walls of partition between us. The emphasis, symbolised by the westward-facing President of the Eucharist, and by the nave altars, is on bringing the Spirit of God into the congregation, rather than on making contact within the

171

chancel and inviting the congregation into the sacred space. This concept means that most parish churches, which are medieval in style, if not in age, do not fit the new pattern of worship and need refurbishing. Their long chancels are unsuitable and represent a largely wasted space. Many of the renewed churches I visited had evacuated the chancel completely as a music group had superseded the choir, and had moved into the nave. The altar had been placed, as Cranmer directed, lengthwise above the chancel steps or in the nave. One church had restored an Elizabethan wooden altar and reading desk that had been put into a side chapel, to what was probably its original position at the top of the steps from the nave to the chancel; before Archbishop Laud in 1634 decreed that altars should be put back to the east end. Another had blocked off the chancel altogether and turned it into a week-day chapel. But even the stoutest renewalist vicar's heart quails at the turmoil that removing the Victorian pews can cause. One church had turned them round to face the altar on the chancel steps, but had baulked at taking them out. People get passionate about the pews. 'God would be very upset if we moved the pews' said one vicar reporting the views of his Parochial Church Council. Some churches had gone to the extent of replacing pews with seating (but in fact it does not seem to get moved around much, if at all)!

But the significance of this furniture-moving, the meaning of the *sacerdos*, the sacred place, and the altar (where the encounter between God and his people is symbolically acted out) coming down into the heart of the congregation, is only just beginning to emerge. As Graham Kendrick says in his book *Worship*, 'If we are allowing God to do his construction work among us, we can expect to be led into the holy of holies and into an experience of God's living presence right in the centre of our meeting together'. The worshipping congrega-

172

tion becomes the sanctuary, the holy place in which God dwells bodily. But as God comes closer, there is more demand on us to be holy. A new purification, a reconsecration is required. Spiritual renewal is an integral part of the process. The danger of modern renewal of all kinds is superficiality. We can go lightly over our repentance, moral lapses are not so important, we are on a praise level now. In the new liturgy the emphasis on the burden of our sins being intolerable has gone and some feel that there is a need for more emphasis on holiness. We are proclaiming that the Lord is here and announcing the greatness of God, but doubts were expressed to me whether the message that is being proclaimed is really going home. Are people making glib statements without really thinking what they are saying? Or is it that turning away from ourselves, from our self-concern and self-love to the praise of God, to focusing on him, is in itself a *metanoia* that will wither away the root of sin and bring healing?

Renewal of all kinds has touched some people's lives, and this shows in the worship. Liturgical renewal, according to one diocesan missioner, has led to 'In-depth questioning and participation by the laity in the role of the liturgy in their spiritual life'. Spiritual renewal is bringing people who were good churchgoers into a new awareness of God's presence in their lives, bringing about a new dedication and consecration, enabling them (as Bishop Pat Harris said) 'to present their body to God for use in service as a living sacrifice, and that is what real spiritual worship is, not just singing that "Jesus is Lord", though for some this is still too costly and threatening'.

A new sense of the dynamic presence of God within the congregation leads to anticipation about what God is going to do next. Bishop Pat Harris described the atmosphere in the church before the services as being electric, like in a theatre when you are waiting for the

173

curtain to go up. 'What is going to happen? Not just "Let's get through the service, p. 119 in the ASB" or whatever, but a sense of anticipation. Somehow there is an electric presence there because the Holy Spirit is with us, and we are never quite sure what he might do, God is going to speak. How is he going to meet us tonight?'

The shift in the whole Church towards a more sacramental Eucharist-centred worship has produced a mixed reaction. The service of the Eucharist incorporates within itself all the elements required for the spiritual renewal of the Church, and many welcome its coming to the forefront of parish worship. Others are worried by what they see as a trivialising of the sacrament; they feel that people are not preparing themselves as they used to, that it has become just part of the regular routine of Church life, instead of the special encounter with Christ that was once carefully prepared for, and looked forward to. Many worshippers today rarely attend any service other than Holy Communion, and there is some criticism that the sermon alone cannot provide enough teaching. A further problem is that the Eucharist excludes the fringe. It is for the in-group, but there is a need also for more open, missionary services to which outsiders can be invited. There is also a need to provide for the children, who can feel excluded by this totally adult-oriented service. At one parish I visited I was told of a family who had moved to a neighbouring parish and had attended the church there, but had found that everyone was expected to attend a Parish Eucharist at which no provision was made for the children, and no concession made to the fact that they were there. The children objected strongly to going to this church, and as they did not wish to put the children off going to church permanently, the family commuted back to the parish from which they had come, where provision was made (much to the children's relief). 'We are never going back to that other place again' said the children firmly. Such incidents produce eclectic congregations. On the other hand, a family Eucharist I attended, which was a big growth-point for the church concerned, would not have been tolerated by many traditional churchgoers. Although a crèche was provided for babies, together with activities for the children, some parents preferred to keep their children with them, and we were surrounded by babies and toddlers who became increasingly tearful as the service progressed. The service was, as the vicar himself said, somewhat rough at the edges. Trying to cater for any one group will alienate the others, who will vote with their feet and not come, unless they too are given provision; but splitting the congregation is still looked upon in some churches as an intolerable option.

I found it surprising that in talking to many clergy and lay people all over the country, of every kind of churchmanship, only one person actually alluded to the total experience of the Eucharist as an ongoing form of spiritual renewal. Perhaps this was taken for granted, but in view of the restlessness and dissatisfaction in the Church today over our corporate Church life (particularly over worship) assumptions need to be questioned. Most people think of the spiritual life as a very slow ongoing growth, in which the nourishment of the Eucharist plays a fundamental role. But is this spiritual growth bringing about the radical change and the submission to the rule of the Kingdom that the Gospel demands? If, as Graham Kendrick suggests in theory, we are in practice:

1. Entering his gates with thanksgiving and praise.
2. Bringing a sacrifice of praise, self-offering, giving to God.
3. Remembering his goodness.
4. Being cleansed and consecrated.

175

5. Coming into unity with one another.

6. Enlightened by the Holy Spirit to understand the word of God.

7. Being caught up in the intercession of Christ on our behalf.

8. Worshipping and adoring God beyond the veil.

9. Resting in Christ's completed work.

10. Feeding on Christ.

11. Partaking in the power of his resurrection.

12. Communing with the Father.

13. Joining the praises of heaven ...

... If we are doing all this, how can we fail to be renewed? If ongoing renewal is not taking place in the Eucharist, then it suggests that there are blocks that are not being dealt with. Is it lack of penitence, as some have suggested, lack of challenge, overfamiliarity, is it the desire to jog along without any real *metanoia* taking place, is it due to a lack of expectation that God can and will continue to work powerfully in our lives, even after conversion or commitment to the Christian life, or is it that a deep insecurity is preventing people from opening their lives up to the transforming power that is there?

How much the cutting edge of the Gospel is being presented, and whether or not it is being received, is a perennial problem for the Church. The whole point of liturgical renewal was to present the Gospel in a modern way so that it could be heard, to do away with the non-verbal message that God was in the past and irrelevant to life today. A bishop said to me that he thought that liturgical renewal had been generally accepted, but I found that it was encountering considerable resistance. 'Liturgical renewal causes painful division amongst congregations, sometimes bringing about learning, sometimes even more division', commented a diocesan missioner. Nowhere in the Church's life do we see more starkly the division between those who look for stability, permanence, historicity, a championing of old and trusted values, and those who want to break out of the old mould into a modern and dynamic Gospel for today and into an experience of real corporateness in worship, Graham Kendrick is uncompromising:

> If we are to make progress in our worship, there is no escaping the prospect of change. With change comes conflict, and we are afraid of both. If, however, we want to avoid change and conflict, then we must of necessity avoid Christ as well, because his Kingdom only grows as his people radically change to become like him, and the stronger it gets, the more it conflicts with rival Kingdoms, whether of men or of Satan.

But ...

> ... We must be careful not to change the externals before people's own experience of God has been renewed. Worship should develop alongside spiritual growth.

The outer form of worship can only come alive for each member of the congregation, if it corresponds to their inner reality. How do you hold the fellowship together but move it on without going too fast or too slow, into greater freedom and *koinonia*? As Martin Thornton says, the effectiveness of liturgy depends on the creative spirituality of each member of the congregation. If such effort is expended on liturgy and preaching, why has so little been given to developing the life of prayer?

But even in a religious community that is giving itself full-time to prayer, the business of working out how to renew its corporate worship can produce difficulty and tension, because of different gifts and ways of praying amongst its members. A traditional religious community that I visited which contained a wide cross-section of the Church (members of every kind of churchman-

177

ship, from someone of Baptist background, to the most high Anglican, Charismatics, non-Charismatics, traditionalists and liberals, with different kinds of vocation from the apostolic, to the monastic, to the hermit) had been considering how best to renew their corporate worship. They had worked in small groups, where everyone could have her say, and had gone through everything they were doing, asking themselves whether it was authentic, whether it was real for them today, whether it facilitated their task; if not, they would discard it. For example, they discussed the Holy Hour which was held every Friday. For many this was the most difficult and painful hour of the week. Some were not sure why they were doing it, though they had been told in the novitiate that it was important. It was explained that it was a response to Christ's request to his disciples in Gethsemane to watch with him for an hour; in contemporary terms this was seen as a sharing with Christ in the pain of the world today. They decided that if they were meant to be sharing in the pain of the world, then it was right that the prayer time should be painful and difficult, and they went on doing it, but with a renewed sense of purpose. They had been influenced by the Charismatic Movement in the seventies, and had introduced a time of spontaneous worship; but they decided that they had worked their way through that phase, and that what they really wanted to do was to update the Divine Office in its language, so that they could feel more comfortable with their liturgy, and this they have now done.

The problem of attempting to renew our corporate worship is a dual one—the need to develop and nourish individual spirituality, and then to co-ordinate it within the congregation so that individuals of differing gifts, temperaments and ways of praying can offer their worship as a praying body. Some people operate entirely on an intellectual level, and for them

178

the structure of the liturgy and the preaching will be of prime importance. Others of a more 'feeling' type will be led towards affective prayer, and will value the singing, hymns of adoration and praise. Many modern choruses are an invitation to affective prayer, and their mantra-like repetitiousness is a vehicle for devotion. Intuitive people are interested in the facts behind the facts, they are drawn towards contemplation. Waiting on God, being with him, looking at him, listening to him, is their way to worship. Others respond most keenly through their senses, and for them worship will speak and be experienced and be expressed in that way. Art, religious symbols, liturgical dance, bodily gestures will stimulate and help the expression of their worship. We all possess and can exercise all of these attributes, but in practice most people tend to develop one of these functions predominantly. A balanced pattern of worship will incorporate something from all of these elements.

Can the Church of England accommodate within its corporate worship the new Puritan and the sensate, the intellectual and the affective, the traditionalist and the renewalist, the poetic and the plain, the stoic and the passionate, the contemplative and the activist? Each has his or her own gift to bring to the Church, but each tends to be intolerant of the other. They have traditionally taken refuge from one another in polarised churchmanship groups, but the traditional groupings are shifting and no longer fit the bill. One can find oneself nearer to the same sub-grouping in another denomination than to a fellow-Anglican. In the renewed churches I visited, I found renewalist refugees from other denominations. The divide between traditionalist and renewalist goes right across all the churches.

Institutionally the Church of England has developed the intellectual aspect of its worship. It has concen-

179

trated on producing a structured liturgy. Anglo-Catholicism has traditionally provided a place for the sensate in worship, but a need is being felt in other parts of the Church for a broadening of style. Some Evangelicals told me that the most fulfilling corporate worship they had experienced was among Anglo-Catholic Charismatics, who combined the sensate and 'feeling' aspects of worship with the liveliness and participation of the modern renewal. Many churches that are not in the Charismatic Movement are taking on Charismatic styles of worship, particularly music, drama, art. 'They may still hate us', one Charismatic said to me, 'but they are singing our songs'.

We seem to have got bogged down in questions of style, and whether people like it or not. Because the modern renewal movements present themselves in modern dress, they are often dismissed as trivial. They lack the rich patina of the archaic. The liturgical renewal aimed at simplicity of expression—but it was too simple, it lacked poetry and was resisted as being banal. The Charismatic Renewal uses modern forms of expression, and is dismissed by some as a merely cultural phenomenon. The driving force behind it, the call to deeper commitment and openness to God, is not heard by those who dislike its style. If you dislike singing choruses, you cannot take seriously people who do.

Music is a very sensitive area. For many of the congregation it is the main point at which genuine participation can take place. Some people want nothing but hymns from Ancient and Modern all the time, some want Charismatic choruses, some want anthems, others do not. The attempt to achieve a cultural mix produces grumbles after every service; it was either too modern, or too old-fashioned. The choir is often one of the first casualties of renewal. In a reverse of the marvellous account in Hardy's *Under the Greenwood Tree*, where he describes the small chamber music group being ousted by the choir and the organ in Victorian times, the choir and the organ are now being overtaken by music groups with their guitars. In one parish I visited a pitched battle over modes of worship centred on the choir, who had dwindled in number to four members, and who sat in the chancel glowering every time a modern hymn or chorus was introduced. The choir was dead, but it would not lie down until it was sacked and replaced by a music group, who are now an established and popular part of the worship. One choir that was sacked by a Charismatic church has stayed in being and hires itself out to churches that want its services. It is very popular.

This stumbling over styles has produced a plurality of responses to the services and music now available for use. The questionnaire I sent to the dioceses showed that most urban churches use the Alternative Service Book, but rural churches on the whole are more conservative and prefer the Book of Common Prayer. Many parishes use both, using BCP or Rite B for their elderly congregations, and Rite A for the growing number of young families who come to the Parish Eucharist. When I visited parishes, I was subjected to such a variety of services that I firmly clutched the book or leaflet proffered to me at the door, unsure what to expect. Even in what appeared to be a Series 3 booklet would lurk the vicar's own version, pasted over the original and accepted by the congregation, but a trap for the unwary visitor like me. I encountered among Anglo-Catholics a crossbred version of the Anglican and Roman rite, and some were using the Roman Daily Office, which is more varied and interesting than the ASB Morning Prayer. At the Loughborough Conference of the Anglo-Catholic Renewal movement in 1985 participants were offered a choice of Daily Office between BCP, ASB and the Roman rite. Most opted for the Roman rite. Among Evangelicals I found that many were using the excellent Family Service produced by CPAS. Family Services are the big growth-point in many parishes, but they need an approachable liturgical style, and some Evangelical parishes have found that the CPAS Service fits the bill. Charismatics are writing their own Guest Services, more open informal services aimed at the newcomer. These have a very slight liturgical content, with an emphasis on singing and preaching, very much 'early Methodist' in style. A typewritten leaflet was a welcome alternative to skimming through a variety of booklets and hymn books— in one church I was presented with a veritable library. At Lee Abbey (one of the first communities dedicated to the renewal of the Church to come into existence after the war) the community shares its renewed worship with visitors, many of whom are experiencing this for the first time. The worship reflects the influence of the Liturgical Renewal, the Charismatic Renewal, and the Meditation Movement. In the morning they make the most of the flexibility of Rite A (ASB), but they stick to the structure. Before lunch they have a more open Charismatic style of worship, made up of praise and singing. In the evening they have 'Christ in quiet' which (as the name suggests) is a time for silence and meditation, with some music. Visitors frequently say, 'This is a touch of heaven', and the community is concerned to say to them, 'God is where you are too, how can this become part of your worship?'

There is a growing demand for spontaneity, participation and silence in worship. There is certainly much more lay participation in services than there used to be, but the fuller participation that many lay people are wanting can only really take place in small groups, not led by the vicar, because the presence of the professional is an inhibiting factor. Only a few clergy are trusting enough to allow spontaneity in the bigger service—freedom of expression is generally left to the informal house group. Silent prayer is even harder to come by. The intuitive/contemplatives have a job to find a home and often have to come out into the Meditation Movement to find corporate expression for their worship. I was told of a Lent series on prayer at which the participants kept on coming back and back to the same question: 'Would it be awkward to be in silence together?' 'Is it possible to have corporate silent prayer, not just on your own?' There has been a growth in the number of groups coming together for silent worship, such as the Fellowship of Contemplative Prayer, and the Julian meetings. Contemplative prayer has an added strength when it is done as a group activity. When Hilary Wakeman, the founder of the Julian meetings, wrote to the *Church Times* suggesting a Julian society, she was inundated by letters from people saying that they wanted to meet for silent prayer. Groups have sprung up all over the country, but Hilary Wakeman says, 'I look forward to the day when Julian meetings are no longer necessary, because people in every parish will be meeting together for silent prayer'.

How much of our very real differences can we transcend, in order to come together as Anglicans in a local community to worship God in a way that is authentic for all who are taking part? We seem to be able to strike the right note on the grand State occasion, but at parish level we are having difficulty in expressing our corporate soul; we seem to be catering for one group to the exclusion of another. Is it possible, asks Phil Bradshaw, Convenor of the Community of Celebration, in their newsletter, to have an environment where people of high faith or none will feel equally accepted at a human level, and people from different traditions will feel at home because the sense of God's presence among the people is greater than the feeling of religious style? Or is this just a pipe dream?

Should we, as Canon Ivor Smith-Cameron suggests, have a 'cafeteria system', with different kinds of menus for differing needs? The dictum that we must keep the whole congregation together at all times and at all costs seems to be breaking down, with whole groups voting with their feet.

People are certainly shopping around to find a church that they can worship in; but it is the quality of *commitment* that attracts, as well as liveliness in worship, the teaching being given, or the liturgical style.

> It certainly gave me on my first visit the impression that here was a gathering of totally committed Christians who were doing something vitally important.
>
> Is that a Church of England church? They were singing, and laughing and dancing! But they were putting their whole heart and soul into the worship, not just going there because it's the thing to do.
>
> Many of our regular congregation and Council Members are here because when they first came they found God in and through our liturgical style.
>
> It is the teaching that brings me here.
>
> I have been round every church in my area, but God has brought me here.

'Many people come to church but are not fulfilled, because they are not ministered to in the power of the Spirit', said a clergyman. But worship is giving as well as receiving; self-surrender brings fulfilment. Those to whom I talked who expressed a sense of fulfilment were those who had been enabled to give themselves most whole-heartedly to God in worship, and I found them in churches that were expecting, and getting, a high level of commitment.

'The Church has unintentionally been infected by secular humanism, which pervades our theology and ethics. In the attempt to identify with non-Christians we have compromised our faith. God is calling his

184

Church back to commitment, to faith in him, to holy living. Hence the emphasis on worship—putting God back into first place. We are being called into an intimate relationship with God, which in turn means right doctrine and right living.' The curate who said this is sounding a note that you will hear in parishes that are experiencing spiritual renewal. Worship is a priority which comes alive as people enter into a deeper surrender to the claims of Christ. A new confidence and joy in corporate worship emerges as people come out from behind their fences to participate with one another, and to encounter the living God who is there among his people.

Fifteenth-century English religious art reflects this same feeling. The painted figures in stained glass or fresco exude an air of quiet jubilation. They do not shout or brandish like the figures on the ceiling of the Sistine Chapel, rather they give an impression of subdued but joyful order. God is in his heaven, and men and women, saints and angels are going about their appointed tasks in a sober and absorbed, yet confident and happy mood which is characteristic of the English spirit at its most fulfilled. I found this English spirit breathing through the externals of worship in conservative and modern settings. Modern renewal is a chameleon, and takes on the colour of the local scene. Though young people today are used to a Transatlantic culture, Charismatic Renewal in particular is becoming less of an American cultural import, and taking on a more authentically English expression.

The new liturgy was made simple so as to be more comprehensible, as though that was all that mattered; but it is an intellectual and dry skeleton, a scholarly structure that can be brought to life only alongside an awakening of the heart and spirit. It lacks the masterly evocative quality of Cranmer's language, the literary art that evokes images in the mind. But where there is a

185

renewed structure and renewed spirit, together with a vivid use of the creative arts to stimulate the imagination, modern liturgy springs to life, bringing both a sense of God's presence, and a release of the spirit of the people in worship. And this, for most people, is more important for fulfilment than intellectual understanding (which is not meant to imply that they are not capable of understanding, but rather that they are looking for more than that). A sense of holy freedom was expressed to me by those who had been enabled to lift mind and heart and spirit to God. For them the reconciliation of the disparate elements had taken place, enabling true worship to be offered.

Worship is the centre—everything else is the outflow.

Jesus himself is coming among his people, and revealing himself by his presence.

The renewal has lifted us above our hobby-horses, into a real experience of living worship.

DETAILS OF SOURCES QUOTED

Jubilate—Theology in Praise: Daniel W. Hardy and David E. Ford. Darton, Longman and Todd, London, 1984.

'Pax' by Joan Brockelsby from *Step into Joy*, Stainer and Bell Ltd, London.

Worship: Graham Kendrick. Kingsway Books, Eastbourne, 1984.

The Heart in Pilgrimage: Father Christopher Bryant SSJE. Darton, Longman and Todd, London, 1980.

Newsletter, June 1985: Community of Celebration.

The Song of the Bird: Anthony de Mello SJ. Image Books, Doubleday, New York, 1984.

Chapter 8

WHAT NEXT?

A pilgrim Church is one which has feet for walking, and is always setting off into the future. So this Church is always revising its style of life, always undergoing a process of renewal, always questioning every step it takes so it never grows old and rusty. The oil which keeps its gears in working order is made up of two things, the Gospel and life itself, that is to say, the words of Jesus and the events and situations which reality goes on putting in front of us. ('The Church the People Want': Document from the Archdiocese of Vitoria, Brazil, quoted in *The Church in the Home*: David Prior. Marshall Paperbacks).

'You've drawn the Church up to the year 2000'. A representative of Roman Catholic youth looked at me unbelievingly. 'The Church won't be there in the year 2000', she insisted. I felt that I had my back to the wall in more ways than one. 'The Church goes on no matter what', said I defiantly. This was 1965, the time of Vatican-II, and in teaching the history of music in a Roman Catholic school, in describing the role that the Church had played in the patronage of music, I had unwittingly stumbled on a burning issue. I told the nun in charge of the class afterwards what had been said. 'That's my form all over', she replied, 'they say "This is all very nice, and we'll come and see you in a museum some day!" ' The devoted efforts of the nuns who were

189

running the school were being dismissed by the young people as totally irrelevant to life as it is lived today.

I had the privilege of working with that religious community both before and after Vatican II, and I saw at first-hand the gentle revolution that renewal brought to its life. I admired the courage, candour and humility with which the nuns faced what they felt to be their failure in mission, their inability to communicate the heart of their life to the next generation, and their willingness to change their style completely in response to that challenge. It was my first introduction to issues of renewal, at a time when the Church of England as I knew it was showing very little sign that it was willing to address the contemporary situation. I wondered then whether my own Church would ever have the courage and confidence to go through a similarly rigorous self-examination.

Fifteen years later, I found myself a partner in the national Partners-in-Mission Consultation. It was not exactly the Church of England's Vatican II, but it was the first attempt that the Church had made nationally to undertake some kind of analysis of its effectiveness in mission, with the help of partners from overseas. The Church was still there, but reduced to the faithful remnant, who were endeavouring bravely to hold the line in a world turned pagan again. A process of national self-examination has begun, and has been taking place sporadically all over the country in the dioceses, as they take part in similar exercises; and it is beginning to happen at parish level, as parishes take part in mission audits. Although change has not been rapid, new developments have been simmering away quietly, and I found a yeasty fermentation growing among lay people in particular, as spiritual renewal reaches them.

Brother Roger of Taizé has declared that we are now

experiencing a spring-time in the life of the Christian Church. In this century the spiritual climate of Western Europe has gone through a long, cold, dark winter, shadowed by two world wars whose wounds have been slow to heal. Scientific materialism and secular humanism have sapped the foundations of Christian faith. But in the Church one can now see signs of new life and growth. However cold it still may be, the indications are with us that spring is here.

When the Partners-in-Mission Consultation in the Church of England took place in 1981, the overwhelming impression that the overseas partners gained by their visits to parishes was of empty churches. But this is not the whole picture. Since the 1960s a quiet fermentation has been taking place with a gathering momentum, and is now beginning to come to the fore. A diocesan bishop said to me, 'When I first came to this diocese five years ago I felt that you could count on the fingers of one hand the people who were really praying. But that has changed; there is a new confidence and prayerfulness, a spiritual lightening of the atmosphere'. A bishop from overseas visiting this country after a gap of several years remarked, 'There is a spiritual awakening among some people in the Church here that I did not see on my previous visit—a certainty that was not there before, or which I did not perceive'. A new confidence and vitality is to be found in the Church, and within this the renewal movements, the Charismatic movement, the Cursillo movement and the Meditation movement, seem to act as catalysts which accelerate the rate of development. My researches showed (and a questionnaire to the dioceses in 1984 seemed to confirm) that between 10 and 20 per cent of parishes are undergoing some form of renewal (approximately 7 per cent of these are in Charismatic renewal), though the proportion varies from diocese to diocese, and the edges of renewal are fuzzy and difficult to delineate.

Some churches have been experiencing renewal for a number of years now, and the impact is there for us to see.

The church is beginning to show signs of new life, and in the country as a whole there is a new openness to the Gospel—people are losing trust in humanist solutions and turning to God. But the institutional Church is desperately slow in responding, and gives the impression of not having yet got to grips with the situation. We need to embark on a process through which the whole Church—not just those in the renewal movements—starts to take renewal issues more seriously, and puts them wholeheartedly at the centre of its agenda, instead of striving so hard to keep the status quo going that renewal becomes merely a fringe activity.

The Church of England is now showing more confidence in facing the challenge of crisis, in playing her part in putting her house in order, and in the renewal of society. At a grass-roots level individual elements in the Church are already doing so, but until the gifts of the whole Church are employed in the task, we will not see the kind of renewal that so many people are longing for. Lambeth '88 will address the theme of *The Renewal of the Church for Mission*, and this may signal the beginning of a more central approach to the issues. But without spiritual renewal, without a renewal of faith and hope and vision, experience seems to show that renewal for mission will remain an unattainable goal that the Church lacks the strength to reach. A feature of those who have experienced spiritual renewal, however, is their confidence that God has put within our reach the resources needed for the task. Their renewed relationship with him has given them confidence and trust to overcome the difficulties with which they are faced, and to find a place of spiritual growth and life. What must not happen is that we

192

simply go on as we are—the crisis is too deep for that, and will not allow us the luxury of inaction.

After a time of research, reading, reflection and writing, I am left feeling both encouraged and challenged. Encouraged by what can be done and by what is happening; challenged by a sense of urgency, because in so many parts of the Church of England more positive things could be happening and are not. I have seen the Gospel being preached to the poor, people finding healing and a new freedom, life and hope. But I have also met those who are searching for what they need, but cannot find in our parishes. Through them I was made aware that there are still too many captives in the pews of our churches, who have come to worship God, but who are hungry and are not being nourished by the Gospel. A lowest common denominator of spirituality will not do for them, for it does not satisfy them. They are hanging on, but not maturing as they should as Christian people. Others have experienced spiritual renewal and want to help others, but are not being properly employed. As one vicar said, 'There is so much to be done that unemployment is a nonsense'. Some churches I visited were good at one particular task, but could not offer the breadth of experience and training that some people needed. For example, some Evangelical Charismatic churches that I visited were very good at bringing in new Christians, both in converting and in initiating them; but after about two years the new converts were becoming restless because they wanted to go deeper into the spiritual life. To do so, some of them were looking to other sources, more impenetrable to outsiders, but concentrating on spiritual maturity. I found that there were few churches that offered the whole range of what people seem to need in their total spiritual journey. The eclectic church has a positive role to play, but I found few clergy who were not defensive about this. The 'parish patch' is still regarded as sacrosanct, although in fact people are 'shopping around' to find the right resource, or the right place in which they can make their contribution. Within the wider Church it is possible to find the right resource or opportunity, if only people knew where to find it. Yet still we work in our isolated boxes, insulating ourselves from one another, struggling with problems that someone elsewhere has probably solved. I wish that I could gather together the people I talked to; what a lot of benefit they would gain from hearing one another, and how they could encourage one another! But people tend to move within the confines of renewal or party networks, and it needs a diocesan or national initiative to enable people to listen to one another across these boundaries.

As I reflect upon the individuals and groups I have met who are on the road of spiritual renewal, five characteristics stand out. They are all aiming at a high level of commitment; they possess the ability to communicate; they are addressing contemporary spirituality; they have a strong sense of confidence in God's purpose; and they relate well both within the Christian community and outside it. Commitment, communication, spirituality, confidence and community seem to be the hallmarks of breakthrough.

An Anglo-Catholic Charismatic vicar I talked to felt that the call to greater Christian commitment gave his parish a cutting-edge, both from the Catholic and from the Renewal point of view. He was ministering in a tightly-knit working-class community that understood commitment. There was commitment to the village, and commitment to the trade union; commitment to the Church was seen in parallel to these two. There was still some 'folk-religion mentality' alongside this; people still talked of the 'squarson' vicar who played cricket, and of the one in the sixties who was always asking for money, but the Church in renewal was now something to belong to, rather than something to support. Sunday worship came first, and although to some this seemed fanatical, nevertheless they came to respect it. On the other hand, the vicar felt that growth in the Christian life should lead us to have more compassion for those not so far along the road. He was suspicious of the House Churches' desire for a 'purer' Church. 'If we are growing in Christlikeness, it isn't just a case of greater victories, but of waiting for the little ones, the ones who can't change. Growth in society means growth in compassion. The Gospel is about forgiven disobedience, it isn't about making it this side of heaven'. Nevertheless the parishioners were thrilled with what they were doing. They were visiting one another, praying with one another, studying the Scriptures together, taking part in house groups, being led into meditation, and finding God in silence. All the marks of contemporary spirituality were there, among very ordinary people in a mining village, in a growing community of committed Christians, who had demanded of the diocese (when asked what kind of vicar they wanted), 'We want a man who knows the Lord and can enable others'.

This cutting-edge that is actively looking for conversion and commitment is important in the present-day climate, when it can no longer be assumed that the tradition is being passed on from one generation to the next, but when the door is more open to evangelism and mission. The traditional pastorally-oriented churches are losing their congregations, but the churches that look for conversion and commitment are gaining converts. A change in policy is required of many parishes, if they are to do more than struggle to survive. The Churches that are growing fastest are the House Churches, but this is for a perfectly discernible reason: they are structured for mission, and they aim for a higher level of commitment in order to attract converts. The biggest change that has to happen in the Church of England is the transition, both in attitudes and structures, from being a Church that caters for those who are perceived to be already Christians, to becoming a missionary Church. David Clark says in *The Liberation of the Church* (p. 156):

> Nothing less than a new, ecumenical, missionary endeavour is required; a new and dynamic missionary movement, a new form of missionary Church, founded on the faith, experience and skill of lay people engaged in every aspect of the life of our society.

My brief does not include the House Churches; but in studying renewal in the Church of England I have been conscious of them in the background, mushrooming away quietly, shadowing my journeys. They were mostly depicted by Anglican clergy I talked to as a lurking presence that gobbled up their dissident or straying flock; or they were seen as overbearing and difficult by those who had come back into the Anglican Church from them disillusioned or wounded. Seeing the real thing in action for myself helped to put into perspective what I had been told, and also cast light on the position of the Church of England today.

The particular House Church that I visited was racially mixed. Half of the members were Afro-Caribbean, and the rest were white, with a sprinkling of Asians. As many Afro-Caribbeans shun a white-led church, the fact that they were obviously happy within its fellowship spoke volumes for the white pastor. The second thing that struck me was how good they were at communication. The guest speaker from Australia combined the skills and flair of the Oriental storyteller with a racy transatlantic style. He took us at breakneck speed through a lengthy exegesis of Psalm 34, which left me feeling breathless, but the rest of his audience were nodding their affirmation. Add to this some

196

deafening music from a pop group, and you have a cultural package which enabled communication to take place with people whom the Church of England would not even be able to touch. As a piece of communication it was as professional as many of the things one sees on television, but with singing, dancing, hand-clapping, cheers, counter-cheers, and laying on of hands it had what television lacks—audience participation. When we got outside, an Anglican friend said, 'Well, if that's how they relate to God, that's all right'. It was not what we wanted from a Church, but we were glad that there was a Church that could reach them with the Gospel.

Where does that leave the Church of England, with its claims to be all things to all men? That universalist kind of Church seems to be quietly dying away, undercut by the inability of individual churches to relate to the whole spectrum of a pluralist society. The attempt to be all things to all men at group or parish level is also failing because we are often weak and compromised by the watering-down of commitment. The Christian communities within the Church of England that are experiencing spiritual renewal are endeavouring in different ways to communicate through a network of relationships in order to raise the level of Christian commitment. They are not trying to accommodate a wide group of people at a low level of spirituality. Spiritual renewal has the effect of moving people who used to be under the Law to an experience of the Gospel. On the communal level this has the effect of changing loosely-gathered groups which are held together by a hierarchy that tried to prevent things going too far off the rails, into more deeply committed, tightly-knit Gospel communities. But these communities tend to be specialist, in that they attract particular sociological groupings. Only on a diocesan or national level can we make any genuine claim to be Catholic in the widest sense of that word, i.e. of encompassing really diverse groups.

Contemporary spirituality, the central issue of renewal, is something that urgently needs to be addressed by the Church. The study of spirituality should not be just a dream in the mind of a Theological College Principal, but a regular part of our daily bread. Wherever I went there were complaints that training, whether clergy or lay, tends to ignore spirituality. Training at national, diocesan and parish level was being criticised for the lack of provision in this area. 'Where is God in all this?' asked a laywoman who had undertaken an otherwise excellent diocesan course in auxiliary pastoral ministry. 'Spirituality is not a special activity for those who like that sort of thing'. Clergy are asking for training in Spiritual Direction, and the courses that are already being provided are over-subscribed.

One vicar was full of praise for the way in which his diocese was facilitating renewal. The bishop had set up structures which had enabled visionary thinking to take place, and this was now percolating down to the parishes. The Bishop's Council had produced seminal documents which had helped to renew the diocese. But he challenged the system of reader training, which was far too academic. It started way beyond where most lay readers were, and therefore it was inappropriate for their needs. He felt that in a working-class situation to say that people could not minister without a knowledge of Church history was nonsense. The lay readers' course was practically useless. He had produced a course to complement it which was, he said, 'Practically wonderful, but academically nowhere'.

This criticism of diocesan lay training as being too academic was a general one. The problem is not only that the courses are not practical enough, but also that the academics are not addressing the right questions.

198

Jürgen Moltmann, a professor of academic theology, says:

> Our academic theology speaks with the Bible, the Church Fathers, and with other sciences and ideologies. But it does not speak the language of the people, and does not express the experiences and hopes of the people. We research the theological concepts of earlier experiences, but we seldom bring the contemporary religious experiences of the suffering or struggling people into new conceptuality. Our theological work thus separates us from the people. Therefore, the people do not understand us, and they view professors and students, even socialist academicians, with deep mistrust.
>
> (*The Open Church*: Jürgen Moltmann, p. 96).

Some of those who are concerned with renewal are beginning to take contextual theology seriously, but this ought to be the rule, rather than the exception that it now appears to be. A typical case of what happens as a result of the exclusion of people's own experience was the woman who was told that she was not academic enough to take the ministerial training course in her diocese and so could not have any kind of ministry in the Church of England (Chapter 3, p. 155). She is in fact a pattern of *diakonia*, the meaning of which is central to the understanding of ministry. Her humble service to her church as sacristan, her caring for the old people to whom she ministers, her ministry of intercession for them and for the Church are all an essential part of that pattern. She leads a prayer group that is praying for the renewal of her Church, and she has been given the gift of tears. She is an example of how the present confusion about lay ministry in the Church of England tends to exclude the more humble, serving, suffering souls who are so precious to the God who reveals himself in Christ.

Those who are involved in clergy and lay training at all levels could take a leaf out of the Cursillo Movement's book, and base their training on the tripod of piety, study and action that Cursillo enjoins people to use as the basis of their Christian life. One falls down without the others; a balance is required, for they are all indispensable aspects of growing in the Christian life. If for piety such training addressed contemporary spirituality, if for study the courses took note of contextual theology, and if for action pastoral skills were practised, this more evenly-balanced diet might begin to give us the wholeness in education and training which today's world requires, and which clergy and lay people would respect.

Contemporary religious experience and contemporary religious movements have often been criticised for being culturally conditioned. But our traditions are culturally conditioned by previous generations, so that they may or may not still seem relevant today. The Church accepts as a norm cultural assumptions that are often Platonist, medieval, eighteenth- or nineteenth-century. Every generation needs to rediscover the essence of the Gospel as something which speaks to its own situation, and needs to discern what belongs to the past, what is cultural conditioning, and what is the Kingdom.

The present tug-of-war about central questions of faith is part of a necessary sorting-out process, in which the experience of those engaged in spiritual renewal will play an increasingly central role. Many of those who have taken the path of spiritual renewal have found that it makes them radical in matters of style, communication and structure, but conservative in matters of faith and doctrine. Bishop Lesslie Newbigin was pointing to this situation as long ago as the 1950s, and today is emphasising that society needs the critique of the Gospel, as well as the Gospel needing the criticism of modern ideas and methods. Christianity flows from a belief in an unbounded God who nevertheless chooses to reveal himself in time and in history. The Church therefore has a prophetic task to discern what he is saying to us today. We cannot but view the revelation of God through contemporary spectacles. However, it is precisely because the mental constructs that we build around our belief have been so stripped down by the changes taking place today, that some people have been going back to the source—the primary experience of the Church, the encounter with God—and are building a construction around that, using the Bible and tradition to interpret that experience, rather than the other way round. This quest for relationship based on *experience*, rather than on *tradition*, is one of the signs of our times that the Church needs to recognise.

'Tell us what the Lord has done for you in the last two weeks, not what he did two thousand years ago', shouted a woman in a crowd to Martin Luther King. Her cry is echoed by our contemporaries. Among the renewal movements there are many prophetic voices eager to tell us what they believe the Lord is doing, from people full of vision, dreams, and artistic expression which seek to articulate an experience which is at a level too deep for ordinary words.

What is certain is that the worldwide ecumenical movements based on spiritual renewal are leading us towards the dual goals of the renewal of the Church, and the renewal of society. Contemplative spirituality, once the preserve of monasticism, is emerging among ordinary people in our congregations, bringing them, and the Gospel, to life. The Charismatic Movement lays a new emphasis on the gifts distributed by the Holy Spirit to the congregation for the building up of the body of Christ, giving a new insight and importance to lay ministry. The Cursillo Movement emphasises the part that every lay person has to play in the mission of the Church, and restores the function of the lay

201

apostolate as the missionary arm of the Church. But while the monastic centres have already begun to respond to the need to pass on their resources to the new lay contemplatives, the rest of the Church has been slow to recognise the significance of these other movements. The Church of England needs to accept the contemporary renewal movements as a sign of our times, and should allocate more of its precious resources of time and people to the study and the application of the new insights that these movements have generated in the world Church.

What is also clear is that the Church and society are at a watershed, a turning-point in their history. The renewal movements are a pointer to this, a sign of something much deeper and wider than is contained within each one of them. When I started, I had some fairly comfortable assumptions about the nature of renewal today. I saw contemporary spiritual renewal (particularly the Charismatic Renewal) as being like the Evangelical Revival and the Oxford Movement, as bringing back into the Church insights and practices which had been lost along the way, and which needed to be restored if the Church was to lead a full Christian life. Though there is an element of such recovery in what is now going on, what I found shattered this cosmetic interpretation, and I became aware of a much deeper, more fundamental shift across the whole Church. There is a struggle to come of age spiritually, a deep desire—particularly among lay people—to take a more active and adult role. This gives many of the livelier parts of the Church an adolescent character. The quest for deeper relationships and the desire for community that are such a striking characteristic of the present situation spring from a need for new ways of belonging in today's society. We need more understanding of the nature of this crisis, and of the significance of the breakthroughs that are being achieved, because we cannot go on ignoring the danger signals that are around. But we need not despair in the face of the difficulties. Spiritual renewal, as I encountered it in this study, is about turning to God and seeking for hidden treasure, for the resources that he provides to enable us to respond appropriately to what he is saying and doing today.

One of our contemporary prophets is Jim Wallis, the American editor of the magazine *Sojourners*. He says:

> The greatest need in our time is not simply for *kerygma*, the preaching of the Gospel, nor for *diakonia*, service on behalf of justice, nor for *charisma*, the experience of the Spirit's gifts; nor even for *propheteia*, the challenging of the King. The greatest need of our time is for *koinonia*, the call simply to be the Church, to love one another, and to offer our lives for the sake of the world.
>
> (*The Call to Conversion*, Jim Wallis)

But what does it mean 'simply to be the Church'? Aren't we doing that now? This statement begs more questions than it answers. *Kerygma, diakonia, charisma, propheteia*, are all part of that meaning, and I found them wherever spiritual renewal was taking place. That Christian love in community that we call *koinonia* is indeed the most precious fruit of the Spirit, the absence of which makes the Church disheartening, but whose presence makes it attractive. Love for the neighbour, and a love for the world that flows from the love of God, are the most mature fruits—the good wine that is poured out in celebration and mission. Their transforming effect can be seen where the process of renewal has been triumphant over difficulties and disasters, to remove the alienation which is at the root of all human sin and which separates us from God. But such love is not automatically produced by the Church—even where renewal was taking place I found cases where love had been sacrificed to lesser gods, where Law had triumphed over Gospel, where

203

clergy and laity had backed away from self-giving in fear, given way to resentment and bitterness, succumbed to the wrong kind of attachment. This showed itself most strongly in the alienation between some people and their leaders. One charismatic leader I spoke to had come to realise that he was blaming all his difficulties on the diocese, and particularly on the bishop. He went to apologise to the bishop, and instead of blaming him talked through his difficulties with him. That was the start of a new and fruitful relationship between Charismatic Renewal and that diocese.

We cannot proclaim liberty to the captives if we ourselves are not free and are not manifesting this kind of love. The institutional Church can be in as much of a bind as secular institutions. We need structure; we need institutions to help equip us, to give us resources for the task. The problem is that at present the institutions are not doing this. The following comment of a Roman Catholic American layman applies to the Church of England as much as to his own Church; but the Church is 'us', not 'them', and in criticising it we can fall into the trap of making it a scapegoat for all our difficulties:

'... in spite of its clear mission, the Church is the largest organisation in the world without goals.'
(*The Lay-Centred Church*: Leonard Doohan, p. 56).

We need to ask ourselves, 'What is the Church for?', and, having answered that question, to sort through what we are doing to see whether it facilitates the task or not. What, then, is the task, and how do we evaluate it?

The Church of England has encountered so much rejection in its recent history that it has (in contrast to the American Church, with its emphasis on success) evolved a theology of failure. It is 'OK' to fail, according to this theology, because Jesus failed, and

went to the cross for it. But no definition of aims, or
success, or failure, is usually given, though success or
failure depends on what the aim is, and whether we
have hit the mark or not. The problem is that our aims
are not clear or defined, and (according to this
theology) neither is God's purpose, so that we cannot
evaluate whether or not he or we are even near the
target.

I found that most lay people I talked to evaluate the
institutional Church, and clergy, quite simply along the
lines of whether they are able to bring them closer to
God or not. The churches that are majoring in spiritual
renewal in its widest sense, are, according to the laity,
much more successful in this task than others. Many
clergy, on the other hand, tend to evaluate success or
failure in terms of the number of people attracted to
the Church, the numbers of new converts, progress in
lay ministry, or vocations to the ordained ministry. In
all these respects the churches in Charismatic Renewal
are the most successful. They are drawing in numbers
of people, bringing those on the fringe to conversion,
making progress in lay ministry, and attracting vocations to the ordained ministry. However, as Bruce Reed
says in his *Dynamics of Religion* (p. 187), 'the task of the
prophet is to evaluate the performance by the Church
of its primary task. He does not judge its effectiveness
by its attendance, spirituality, or the scope of its
activities, which are the measures so often used by the
members of the churches themselves. His yardstick is
the state of the society in which the church works.'
Judged by this yardstick, the churches in the most
deprived areas I visited, which had the most holistic
mission, are succeeding. They are working as agents of
reconciliation among groups of people who are deeply
alienated by our society, and they are bringing a
healing and wholeness which was discernible in a
practical way, such as the building of community and

the stamping out of vandalism. But for the Church of England as a whole, with its pretension to be a State Church, there can be no satisfaction in looking at the condition of our society today; it is demonstrating a crying need for a corporate self-examination.

The style of English society tends to oscillate between the Roundhead and the Cavalier, between repression and permissiveness, in a never-ending attempt to find the right balance. The style of our forbears, which was to keep the lid tightly on, to keep our destructive elements under tight control, to exhort everyone to work hard and be good, and to suppress by rigid discipline all that would not fit into the hard-working, good-living Protestant ethic, led to split personalities and to a split society in which all the tensions that had been suppressed re-emerged in an ill-understood back-lash of sickness and decline in whole areas of our life. Attempts to heal society by simply lifting the lid, on the other hand, opened a Pandora's box of ills. Far from healing the lives of individuals and of society, our actions have brought disintegration into family and community life. Trying to put the lid back on again simply leads to further alienation. What God seems to be doing in spiritual renewal, healing the inner alienation within the psyche and bringing greater wholeness, speaks directly to the heart of the present dilemma of our society.

The Church engaged in renewal resembles a cross between an ambulance station on the margins of society, picking up the casualties of our permissive age, and a kind of Open University for those who are looking for a better answer to the meaning of life than that offered by secular humanism. The Church has in her heart the springs of healing not only for such individuals, but for society as a whole. Nevertheless, renewal remains an infiltration into the fringes of a Church which itself has become a marginal consumer option. If the whole Church is to be more than that, the physician must heal herself. The Church manifests the same deep splits of personality and structure which bedevil our society. We are faced with God-sized problems, for which man-made panaceas and sticking-plaster are not enough. Christian hope springs from what God is doing to overcome our alienation and to restore our relationships.

If Jesus' aim is that described by Isaiah in the 'Suffering Servant' passages (Isaiah 42 ff) then his ministry cannot be said to have failed. A modern version describes God as saying through the prophet in Isa. 52. 13 'My servant will succeed in his task; he will be highly honoured', and in Isa. 53. 10 ff, 'It was my will that he should suffer; his death was a sacrifice to bring forgiveness ... and through him my purpose will succeed ... he will know that he did not suffer in vain. My devoted servant, with whom I am pleased, will bear the punishment of many, and for his sake I will forgive them'.

In this task of restoration and reconciliation the parishes in spiritual and structural renewal are attempting to appropriate this work of Christ, and to help others to do so. I found those who are attempting to restore the Church through spiritual renewal, but who have not dug deep enough into the roots of reconciliation that lie at the heart of the Christian religion, to be frustrated and blaming, still prey to the negativism that infects so much of our Church. Others, like a laywoman who had experienced the lay awakening, was full (as she puts it) 'of a deep joy that never leaves me', and has been called into a ministry of reconciliation—in her case a ministry among drug addicts.

If the purpose of God for the Church is that it should proclaim and continue Christ's work of reconciling the world to God, then our criterion of success or failure will be whether or not what we are doing is overcoming

207

alienation from God. We would see the Church as a Fellowship of Reconciliation, a family of those who have been reconciled to God through Christ, with a mission of reconciliation to the world. This should give us a greater concern about alienation in our own ranks, and a deeper desire for the healing of the Church as well as the nations. The most encouraging thing I experienced on my journeys around the country was to see deep alienation being overcome in many people: the most disheartening was to see alienation within the Church itself, which should rather be the agent of reconciliation. A mark of restoration in the relationship with God is healing in relationships with the neighbour and with society also. For this to happen, as Dr Therese Vanier (who is involved in the hospice movement) says, 'the heart must be touched'. This is the work of spiritual renewal of all kinds: so to touch the heart that our alienation is overcome, and our relationships with God and our neighbour are restored. From alienation, rebelliousness and fragmentation, spiritual renewal is moving people towards restoration, integration and community. If reconciliation with God is the aim, then it follows that this restoration of relationships is the touchstone of success or failure.

With the time and resources available to me I can only begin to scratch the surface of what I found, and to start to turn over the issues in a way that will, I hope, persuade the Church to give more of its precious time, energy and resources to the subject of renewal, and encourage those who are already engaged in it to go deeper. I doubt whether many of those most committed to Charismatic Renewal, for example, have realised the depth of the task to which God is calling them. To have a more holistic view they need to hear what the rest of the Church is saying, and the rest of the Church needs to hear them.

We need also to learn from other Churches. All are

facing similar problems, and all are being affected by the renewal movements. In preparing this study it has been immensely helpful to read widely from work being produced by other denominations. The ecumenical movement seems to have achieved a great deal, but tends to come to a halt against the barriers of traditional denominational structures. I have been on committees and sub-groups of the British Council of Churches for some years, and again and again I have seen initiatives fail when they try to move us together onto ground already occupied by traditional Church work, but succeed when we co-operate on fresh pieces of work concerned with the renewal of Church life and with mission. A good example of successful co-operation has been the recent launching of the 'Not Strangers but Pilgrims' initiative, in which the Churches are working together in self-examination and mission. Co-operation is also fruitful in the area of renewal, since for many people the experience of spiritual renewal has broken the barriers that divide us. In the review of synodical structures that is taking place, the Board for Mission and Unity might be renamed and restructured as the Board for Renewal and Mission, since it is in the wake of renewal that mission and unity—both signs of reconciliation—are being achieved. The emphasis would then be on the horse that is drawing the cart, rather than putting the cart before the horse.

Similarly the Board for Social Responsibility might be reconceived as the Board for the Renewal of Society, since that suggests a more dynamic reform, a renewal which comes as our relationship to God (both as individuals and as a community) is renewed, rather than an ordering of the status quo. What encourages me is that this aim is not a pious hope based on unrealistic expectations, but is something that I have witnessed, something that can happen and is happen-

209

ing in the wake of spiritual renewal. I sum up my reaction to this study in the words of Carlo Carretto from his book *Summoned to Love*:

> Would you like a piece of advice? Don't keep saying 'Everything is about to collapse'. Say, since this is nearer the truth, 'Everything has collapsed already!' You will find it much more cheering and rewarding to think of yourself as building for a new tomorrow, than as defending a past already old and moth-eaten.
>
> 'Let the dead bury their dead' Jesus said Now, 'Go and proclaim the Kingdom'.
>
> And in any case, there is no compelling reason to think that the end of the world has arrived.
>
> We are at the end of an age, and the wonderful thing is that a new age is suddenly beginning, which—in Gospel terms—may well be more fruitful and rewarding.
>
> So try and shed a little of your pessimism.
>
> Try and attend the liturgical assemblies of one or other of the many communities of prayer now springing up like mushrooms throughout the forest of the contemporary Church.
>
> You will find yourself caught up in an explosion of joy and faith rarely to be encountered in the venerable cathedrals of a narrower, more circumscribed age.
>
> And if you do manage to take part in one of these liturgical assemblies devoted to the word of God ... you will certainly come out convinced that the Church is extremely young, and is constantly being reborn from the ashes of her past.

DETAILS OF SOURCES QUOTED

The Liberation of the Church: David Clark. NACCAN.

The Open Church: Jürgen Moltmann. SCM Press.

The Call to Conversion: Jim Wallis. Lion Paperbacks.

The Lay-Centred Church: Leonard Doohan. Winston Press.

The Dynamics of Religion: Bruce Reed. Darton, Longman and Todd.

'The Church the People Want': Document from the Archdiocese of Vitoria, Brazil, quoted in *The Church in the Home*: David Prior. Marshall Paperbacks.

Summoned to Love: Carlo Carretto. Darton, Longman and Todd.

SUMMARY OF
RECOMMENDATIONS

1. Parishes need to address *contemporary spirituality*, and to understand the modern expression of the desire for relationship with God. If the Church excludes the supernatural aspect of faith, people will turn to other bodies—sects, cults and the occult—for its expression. An aspect of contemporary spirituality that parishes should particularly be aware of is the upsurge of contemplative spirituality among ordinary people. They should allow for its expression within parish prayer groups and liturgical activity.

2. The result of renewed spiritual activity among lay people is an increasing emergence of *lay ministry*. Parishes should make lay training a central activity, and clergy should make it a central aspect of their ministry, so as to enable and release the giftedness of individuals for the service of the whole body. Only as the whole body comes to maturity can the Church be rebuilt for mission.

3. Parishes need to become *more missionary* in style, structure and stance. There are tremendous opportunities now opening up for evangelism and mission, but these can be negated by a parish life that is structured around the ministry of one person or of a small group of people only. For mission to be effective the whole

body of Christ needs to be alive, active and welcoming. This transformation can take place as lay people come alive through spiritual renewal, are trained and enabled for ministry, and are supported in that ministry by the whole Church.

4. In order to enable these developments to take place, diocesan and national bodies need to be tuned into contemporary spirituality and its effects on parish life. Clergy and lay training needs to be more holistic. The Cursillo model of piety, study and action is a useful tool to adopt in the form of contemporary spirituality, contextual theology, and training in missionary, as well as pastoral, skills. More clergy need training in spiritual direction, applied theology and evangelism, together with a more holistic sense of mission than is now usual. The lay apostolate needs to be trained and enabled in mission among their family, friends and work relationships. The new models of missionary Church now being built should be studied by the whole Church, and their special leadership needs and skills should be brought to the attention of dioceses.

The shift from a purely pastoral to a more missionary Church brings about structural changes which need to be understood and furthered by all those with responsibility. For example, Church planting is an important area for study, particularly where it cuts across traditional parish boundaries. Present developments, now being monitored by the Board for Mission and Unity, show a need for fresh thinking about our structures, which should enable growth to take place, rather than inhibiting it.

The link between spiritual renewal and mission should be further studied with a view to action at every level of Church life.

5. These developments are ecumenical and worldwide

in their influence, and should be seen and studied in that context. The ecumenical sharing of opportunities and problems in the whole area of the renewal of the Church for mission will enrich and enable the Church.

6. This new thrust should be reflected in the agenda both of the General Synod and of its Boards and Councils. In the current review of synodical structures, the importance of the renewal of the Church for mission and the renewal of society itself should be taken into account. Consideration should be given to re-structuring the Board for Mission and Unity as a Board for Renewal and Mission, recognising that mission and unity now often arise in the wake of renewal rather than vice versa, and that unity may most readily be achieved as the Churches seek to collaborate together in fresh ventures concerned with the renewal of the Church's life and work, particularly with mission. Similar consideration should be given to re-structuring the Board for Social Responsibility as the Board for the Renewal of Society, since this better represents the current task of both Church and society, and their immediate goals.

7. With the time and resources available to me, I have been able only to scratch the surface of the issues, but already I have found much that is both challenging and encouraging. This book should be seen as recording a phase of a process of discovery and evaluation that needs to be continued, rather than a finished conclusion. Further research is needed.

215

APPENDIX

RENEWAL QUESTIONNAIRE

In 1984, a questionnaire was sent to diocesan missioners (or their equivalent) in the Church of England asking for information about the extent and forms of renewal taking place in their dioceses, and about lay participation, training and ministry. Approximately one-third of them responded, and their answers are analysed below.

Although a definition of renewal was given in the introduction to the questionnaire—renewal in relationship to God, the neighbour and in society—and an illustration of stages in renewal in a parish was included (Phase one: renewal of individuals; Phase two: renewal in groups; Phase three: powerful impact upon the structures; Phase four: renewal of the whole parish), many of the respondents had difficulty in answering the questions either because of problems in defining renewal, or because of lack of the necessary information. One missioner sent an interesting run-down of the different perceptions of renewal he had encountered; this was most useful, and has been incorporated in the first chapter of the book. Similar difficulties were encountered in answering the specific question about charismatic renewal. Some saw all renewal as of the Holy Spirit, though not necessarily of the Charismatic movement. Some parishes are charismatic in tone, some have significant charismatic activity within them, and some are firmly within the Charismatic movement. But the difficulties are them-

217

selves illuminating, and in spite of the obvious limitations of the exercise the answers provide a picture of what is happening in at least some of the dioceses of the Church of England. I am most grateful to those who contributed.

RENEWAL EXTENT AND FORM

Question 1.
Please describe, in very general terms, the form or forms which renewal is taking in your diocese.

All answered in terms of *parish* renewal. Form of renewal in order of frequency of mention:

Charismatic, mission, evangelism, prayer and prayer groups, stewardship, parish appraisal, liturgical, ecumenical, small group movement, radical, Cursillo, church growth, study (including Bible study), healing ministry, clergy renewal, lay awakening, spirituality and vision, meditation movement, Anglo-Catholic, Conservative Evangelical, parish missions, quiet days, parish retreats.

Question 2.
Approximately what proportion of the parishes in the diocese would you describe as undergoing renewal?

Answers ranged from 10 per cent to 35 per cent. Average 20 per cent. One said that 45 per cent of parishes were showing 'signs of life'. One answered in terms of the phases of renewal described in the introduction to the questionnaire:

Phase 1 (individuals being renewed) 75 per cent of parishes

Phase 2 (groups being renewed) 45—50 per cent of parishes

Phase 3 (renewal impacting on structures) 20 per cent of parishes

Phase 4 (whole parish renewed) 10 per cent of parishes

OTHER COMMENTS

'General sense of renewal and a feeling that the diocese is "on the Move" '. 'Rural areas slow to change'. The latter was a frequent comment throughout the questionnaire.

218

Question 3
Approximately what proportion of the parishes in the diocese would you describe as undergoing charismatic renewal?

Answers varied from 1 per cent to 33 per cent, average 7 per cent.

Question 4
What changes has the liturgical renewal brought about in the diocese?

Answers in frequency of mention:

More lay participation.

80 per cent now using ASB, but many retain BCP.

New hymns and music, use of choruses and instrumentalists.

More sacramental, Eucharist central, this can exclude fringe.

Increase in community worship.

Redesign of church interiors, nave altars.

Baptism public in most parishes.

Fluctuation showing itself by people seeking out lively churches to worship in.

Laity being trained in leading worship.

Has muted the difference between Anglo-Catholics and Evangelicals.

Relaxation of atmosphere of worship, friendlier.

Urban parishes use ASB, rural use BCP.

Some ASB and participation, others rigid retreat into BCP.

In-depth questioning and participation by the laity of the role of the liturgy in their spiritual life.

Painful division amongst congregations, sometimes bringing about learning, sometimes more division.

Greater emphasis on prayer, both within the liturgy and in informal groups and meetings.

More spontaneity in worship.

Warmer ecumenical spirit.

Westward position adopted by most clergy.

Laying-on of hands for teaching, deliverance.

219

Some liturgical dance.

Rite A becoming norm for Parish Eucharist where the aim is to reach young families. Rite B for the elderly—common pattern is 8.00 a.m., Rite B; 10.00 a.m. Rite A; 6.00 p.m. Evening BCP.

Question 5
Have there been any particular problems associated with renewal in the diocese? If you could provide any specific examples, this would be most helpful.

Answers in order of frequency of mention:

Churches have experienced divisions, some leaving, others joining. One missioner commented, 'There has been a polarisation between "conservative establishment" and the "renewed" group, who declared the rest dull and void—the ensuing confrontation has been schismatic'.

Conservatism—we are reluctant to change.

None.

Tension between clergy and laity, sometimes over baptism. 'In a fair number of parishes lay people in renewal have pressed ahead despite their parish priest, rather than because of him'. Lay participation can cause a sense of clergy crisis, loss of status. Renewal has often taken the form of House Churches which are becoming an increasing problem in splitting Christian communities—and an increasing opportunity of asking why people prefer House Churches (80 per cent of one congregation followed their vicar into a House Church).

Strident demands to use only 1662.

Clergy leaving.

Lay leadership being too authoritarian.
Resentment in some areas to evangelism.
Providing help and advice for those enquiring about Evangelism and leadership for Evangelical teams. Masses of lay people available for evangelistic projects, but leadership scarce.

220

Renewal generally welcome, but some apathy or distaste for change, particularly in rural areas.

Tendency to turn inward in prayer groups.

Family problems—home life being neglected for Church affairs.

Over-expectancy of miracles.

Re-emergence of Evangelical dynamic, causing polarisation between Catholic and Evangelical dynamics, expressed in terms of value and belief systems rather than spirituality.

Question 6
Has your diocese adopted any particular policies with regard to renewal?

Most dioceses responding had no policy. Those which had, responded thus (again, answers in order of frequency of mention):

General encouragement.

Encouragement of Mission Audit or parish appraisal.

Putting in motion the recommendations of a PIM report.

Shared Ministry policy.

'Mission and Ministry study to assist parishes. Some have found new life and confidence through reviewing this, others have backed away—too painful'.

Full backing in every way.

Support of clergy involved in renewal.

Laissez-faire.

'Board of Mission has co-opted the concerns of a group of charismatic clergy in order to keep in touch'.

Appointment of a 'very wise' charismatic as a diocesan exorcist.

Question 7
Is there greater lay participation in the life of the parishes compared with five years ago? Please describe its most significant aspects.

All the respondents answered 'yes' in answer to the first

question. Their description of what is happening is as follows:

There is shared ministry in liturgical roles, pastoral roles and administration. Lay people are helping with visiting, taking the sacrament to the sick at home. Marriage preparation and confirmation preparation.

'There is little doubt that lay people are much more prepared to be involved, and indeed want to be involved with the life of their parishes. Renewal has had a very marked impact in this desire, and as a result, lay people have become both more supportive of their clergy, and also expect more from them. There is a great desire for further ministry and learning in the Christian faith'.

The decrease in the number of priests has served to allow lay participation. Also early retirement and redundancy have made lay people more willing to be used. Some dioceses have developed lay Pastoral Assistants, or have generally encouraged lay participation by diocesan policies, publications, and by residential conferences.

But,

'Parishes find it difficult to give lay people accreditation and space to operate with their training, with notable exceptions'.

'Lay leadership is only emerging slowly in rural areas, far too much is still left to incumbents'.

'Lay Readers feel they are stop-gaps for clergy'.

'It is difficult to conceive the life of a parish without lay participation. It may be better to think of a change in the nature of lay participation. The extent of change is greatly varied. It might be best described as an awareness of responsibility with a wresting of authority from the clergy'.

Question 8
Has there been any significant increase or decrease in the last five years in the numbers of lay people coming in the diocese for:

a) Education and Training?
Most dioceses noted a considerable increase, some an increase, a few were about the same, one had no increase,

222

one noted a decrease, one 'don't know'. Some dioceses mentioned an increase in programmes of education and training.

b) Lay Ministry?
Most dioceses noted an increase, some a considerable increase, two no increase. One diocese commented that their LNSM numbers were burgeoning, and that the numbers of women coming forward for ministry had increased threefold.

Question 9
Could you say what initiatives the diocese has taken with regard to lay ministry?

The answers to this were varied but overlapping:

Creating new posts for Deaconesses.

Encouragement of lay training and ministry.

Bishop's Certificate.

Radio courses.

LNSM.

Appointing a full-time Laity Development Officer with part-time Officers appointed in each Archdeaconry, and a Resource Team to promote Continuing Ministerial Education and Laity Development.

Nothing significant.

Shared Ministry Project (taken up so far by eight parishes).

Separating Lay Ministry from the Ordained in the Structures.

Formation of Ministry Teams.

Training Institute.

Lay conference—had quite an effect!

Considering the matter in Committee.

Being thought about.

Launching a vigorous scheme for lay training.

Appointment of a Ministry Development Officer.

Development of lay ministry is part of diocesan strategy, but I would not say that it amounts to a programme in itself.

Development of a training course open to all, part of Readers' training and that of potential candidates for the ordained ministry.

Pastoral assistants.

Courses for Churchwardens, Readers, Treasurers, Sunday School Teachers.

Training schemes for lay ministers, lay pastors.

Some have found the lay Ministerial Course too academic though most welcome the chance to gain a deeper understanding of the Christian faith.

PIM Lent Course.

Deanery Training Schools; subject 'The Living Parish' including worship, House Groups, Shared Ministry, Sharing the Faith. Sixteen people (lay and clergy) have been trained and are available in teams of four to head the training schools throughout the diocese.

Question 10
Are there any further comments that you would wish to add to this enquiry?
The answers were various, and I quote:

'Some Deaneries within the diocese have active Mission Committees which encourage renewal'.

'Some clergy have benefited from Anglican Renewal Ministries Conferences'.

'The Diocesan Missionary Council puts on "Mission Today" evenings, mostly to do with overseas mission, but one evening they considered mission within the parish, and church growth'.

'On the whole, renewal has been a thoroughly positive element in the life of the diocese, and is now well integrated into it. It no longer has the slightly exotic and strange flavour that was true some years ago, and although there have been casualties, it feels a good deal more Anglican than it used to'.

'It would take rather a long time to analyse the situation in this diocese. There is a fairly clean divide between the small minority (10 per cent) who experienced charismatic renewal several years ago; a middle section (30 per cent) where new patterns of worship and personal commitment have broken through, and the rest who remain fairly unchanged'.

'I guess we are a very conservative diocese. The clergy can have super ideas but they do not take off, or encouragements pass down from Bishop's Council, BMU, etc., but are "sat on" by incumbents. Some clergy and lay people have made great steps forward, but there is always the danger of splintering off into House Churches'.

'It might be helpful to define the task of Renewal. The definition of parish renewal sounds like Margaret Thatcher's programme'. 'During 1984 a group has been set up informally to plan a programme of Charismatic Renewal at diocesan level!'

So far there has been a day led by the Bishop of Pontefract with about 180 people attending. Two study days on the Holy Spirit led by Canon John Finney. In 1985 there is to be a 'Pentecost Praise' in the cathedral, a weekend Conference at the Retreat House and a day meeting. A clergy fellowship now meets. The prayer meeting in the Cathedral once a month is attended by about 20 people.